A Quick Guide to Writing Business Stories

Business journalism is of critical importance to society, though it may appear to some that it concerns only big business and big investors. *A Quick Guide to Writing Business Stories* helps students acquire the marketable writing skills required to succeed in this competitive and vibrant segment of print and online journalism. This hands-on, practical text provides step-by-step guidance on how to write business articles such as the corporate quarterly earnings story, small business profiles, and business or consumer trend stories.

Mathewson's book, based on Northwestern University's highly successful business journalism program, guides students in the use of data, documents, and sophisticated expert sources. With *A Quick Guide to Writing Business Stories* as their resource, students will be able to write challenging stories with clarity and speed, greatly enhancing the journalist's ability to tackle stories on other complex topics, in any medium.

Joe Mathewson reported on business and law for *The Wall Street Journal* and has taught business reporting and writing at Northwestern University's Medill School of Journalism, Media, Integrated Marketing Communications since 1997. He has practiced law, covered the U.S. Supreme Court for *The Journal*, and is the author of *The Supreme Court and the Press: The Indispensable Conflict* (2011).

A Quick Guide to Writing Business Stories

Joe Mathewson

NEW YORK AND LONDON

First published 2016
by Routledge
711 Third Avenue, New York, NY 10017

and by Routledge
2 Park Square, Milton Park, Abingdon, Oxon OX14 4RN

Routledge is an imprint of the Taylor & Francis Group, an informa business

© 2016 Taylor & Francis

The right of Joe Mathewson to be identified as author of this work has been asserted by him in accordance with sections 77 and 78 of the Copyright, Designs and Patents Act 1988.

All rights reserved. No part of this book may be reprinted or reproduced or utilised in any form or by any electronic, mechanical, or other means, now known or hereafter invented, including photocopying and recording, or in any information storage or retrieval system, without permission in writing from the publishers.

Trademark notice: Product or corporate names may be trademarks or registered trademarks, and are used only for identification and explanation without intent to infringe.

Library of Congress Cataloging in Publication Data
Names: Mathewson, Joe, 1933- author.
Title: A quick guide to writing business stories / Joe Mathewson.
Description: New York ; London : Routledge, 2016. | Includes bibliographical references.
Identifiers: LCCN 2015048430 | ISBN 9780765646217 (hardback)
Subjects: LCSH: Journalism, Commercial—Handbooks, manuals, etc.
Classification: LCC PN4784.C7 M28 2016 | DDC 808.06/665—dc23
LC record available at HYPERLINK "https://protect-us.mimecast.com/s/zNXlBdU0b1nLhD" http://lccn.loc.gov/2015048430

ISBN: 978-0-7656-4621-7 (hbk)
ISBN: 978-1-315-72021-0 (ebk)

Typeset in Times New Roman
by diacriTech, Chennai

Contents

	Introduction	1
1	Why Business Journalism?	5
2	Words	8
3	Numbers	21
4	People	31
5	The Earnings Story	37
6	Financial Services Reporting	44
7	The Corporate Finance Story	50
8	The Bankruptcy Story	54
9	The Corporate Outlook Story	60
10	The Economic Indicator Story	69
11	The Small Business Story	74
12	The Trend Story	80
13	The Consumer Story	83

vi *Contents*

14	The Derivatives Story	88
15	The Agriculture Story	96
16	The Sports Business Story	101
17	The Energy Story	104
18	The Not-for-Profit Story	107
	Conclusion: You're Important!	111
	Works Cited	118
	Appendix	119
	Index	121

Introduction

Your future in business journalism will be a big responsibility, and your effort to get it right starts with your decision about what to cover. Your judgment matters. Among the daily cascade of data and words about business and the economy, there are worthwhile stories, but inevitably there's also dross. It's obvious that you'll write about gross domestic product and the consumer price index and the unemployment rate when they're released. But it's not so obvious that you'll give much attention to a release of the chain deflator or the employment cost index, unless you're writing for a specialized publication. And then there are your own story ideas, with their competing claim for your time and output.

This daily sorting-out process is inefficient. Some starts will produce only a stop. Fortunately journalists, even those who write about production efficiency, aren't rated on their own efficiency. Speed, yes, but not efficient use of time. Even if you've studied accounting or economics, the judgment needed to make these story decisions is developed only over time in your journalism job, and how long that time is depends in part on how much you read about the economy and in particular your own beat. If you keep an eye on *The Wall Street Journal, Financial Times, Bloomberg BusinessWeek* and other fine business publications, you'll get a sense of what's important, what knowledgeable folks are talking about.

However, don't confine yourself to what other business journalists are writing. Read the data yourself, and when you have a notion that there's an uncovered story there, try it out on your editor, or a securities analyst or an economist. And don't be discouraged if they tell you you're all wet. That's part of the continuous, necessary process of trial and error, of pushing and probing, of testing and trying. The journalists who have the most *bad* story ideas are among the *best* journalists, for they have the *most* ideas, a few of which will be excellent.

Once you've got a story in hand, whether it's from a release or your own enterprising, then there's another judgment call: what facts, what data, what expert quotes, what examples are needed to tell that story? At first, a prescient editor can advise on this. In time you'll come to make your own determinations. That sounds simplistic, and in a sense it is.

Because there's no formula for making such judgments, any more than there's a formula for judging the relative worth of stories. It comes with experience, sometimes fairly rapidly, and it's part of what makes business journalism such delicious, challenging and gratifying work. Crafting the stories described in this book will give you the hands-on experience and confidence level to move comfortably into first-rate jobs.

"It's Not News If It's Not True"

That's what Matt Winkler, founder and longtime editor-in-chief of the time-sensitive Bloomberg News service, likes to tell Bloomberg's 2,300 reporters and editors. For Bloomberg, with its worldwide audience of investment professionals and business executives, both speed and accuracy are absolutely essential. A later correction doesn't help the trader who just lost money in the stock market because of a wire-service mistake or misplaced journalistic emphasis on misleading numbers in a company's earnings announcement. And those announcements are often distorted these days, to make a company's results appear much better than they actually were. In other words, to hide the truth, which is still the journalist's lodestar. It can't be compromised by the need to hurry, to beat the competition.

Similarly, there's competition to report important government data, such as the monthly unemployment rate. These figures, too, can move markets, meaning investors, hedgers and speculators can make or lose money depending on how they've placed their bets on this particular statistic. If you must get the number out immediately, tack on as soon as possible interpretive quotes from economists, analysts or other experts. If they should undermine the face-value authenticity of the new number, or even scoff at it, you'll want to rewrite your lede as well as insert some skeptical quotes high in the second version of your story.

When you cover a speech, perhaps by a prominent, authoritative person, interview a few audience members immediately afterward. (Double-teaming this story can be very helpful.) How did the words sit with them? A mind-changer? Helpful? Questionable? Waste of time? Whatever, put a listener quote or two high in your story, and perhaps reflect the predominant reaction in your lede, particularly if it's negative, such as: "The Secretary of Commerce delivered an unexpectedly gloomy assessment of the economic outlook, to the dismay of her business audience."

The Man on the Street Can't Be Wrong

When writing an economic indicator story, if you have the luxury of getting out on the street and interviewing passers-by about their economic lives, by all means do it. And don't assume the stats are right and your interviewees should be simply a humanized confirmation of the release. For instance, if a national survey says consumer confidence is rising, but local consumers tell you they're discouraged and depressed, don't kick yourself for picking atypical people. They are what they are. They're genuine. And depending on how many people you've talked to (again, double-teaming is good, *especially* if you're interviewing on camera), recognize their pessimism high in your story, maybe even in the same breath as the national statistic.

A Story Based on Doubt

Despite the inescapable need for data in business journalism, there's a place for a story about doubt, typically starting with your own doubt. If you, in your substantial wisdom, are wondering whether the stock market can keep rising indefinitely, this may be a doubt you can hang a story on. Of course you need to find other doubters, perhaps even more authoritative than you. Among professional people like economists and analysts, there are always doubters or skeptics. This is not to suggest that you fake a contrarian story simply by quoting a few outlying naysayers, especially if they've been consistently and recently wrong. But if the doubters can cite history, data and trends that strike you as substantive, responsible and thus worth consideration, that's a valid story. Write it. With appropriate recognition of the prevailing majority view, of course.

In journalism there's always room for more creativity, for greater imagination, for new story ideas, for initiatives both ponderous and entertaining. And because we are all economic creatures, cogs in a vibrant economy the likes of which the world has never seen, there's endless room, indeed need, for solid journalism that will enlighten consumers as well as business people and investors, journalism that will help them to wisdom, success and perhaps even happiness as they wend their economic way through life.

This textbook grows out of teaching a hands-on, very practical business reporting and writing course over the past 18 years at Northwestern University's Medill School of Journalism, Media, Integrated Marketing Communications. Our method works. Students with no prior background, experience or knowledge of business, and no yen whatsoever for math, learn to handle numbers and complex stories with confidence, and to write them clearly and on deadline. Many of those folks are handling business beats these days for Bloomberg News, *The Wall Street Journal,* Reuters, such fine city business weeklies as *Crain's Chicago Business,* the *Philadephia Business Journal* and the *Orange County Business Journal* and other first-rate publications and subscription-only online news services such as Tax Analysts and Reorg Research. The journalism profession, and the American public, need such practitioners.

This book does not purport to teach everything there is to know about business and finance and the economy, a complex and fast-moving world indeed. However, it provides a solid platform on which to build, and to win a job as a business journalist in a high-standards, multimedia organization. These job opportunities are rife these days, and the pay is good. But only a minority of beginning journalists will make the effort to qualify for them.

For the student who chooses not to pursue business journalism, this training in the use of data, documents and sophisticated expert sources, and in writing challenging stories with clarity and speed, greatly enhances the journalist's ability to tackle stories on other complex topics, in any medium. And a general-assignment reporter who can handle a business story occasionally is more valuable than one who can't. Of course, outside journalism the knowledge and skills addressed here can be equally useful—in financial or investor relations and other aspects of financial communications.

For all students, this book will open the door to a gratifying understanding of the world we live and work in. And, believe it or not, gaining this understanding is fun! I require my students to laugh every day, and they invariably have reasons to do so.

Write on!

1 Why Business Journalism?

No other nation in history has achieved the economic success and comfortable standard of living that the United States enjoys today. Business is the essential foundation and driver of modern American life, and our future. Everyone has a stake in our nation's business, for better or worse. Always changing, business is must coverage for responsible journalism, in all media.

Therefore, it follows that business journalism is enormously important to all of us, though it may appear to some that it concerns only big business and big investors. Not so. Two-thirds of our economy, expressed as gross domestic product, our total output of goods and services, is driven by consumer spending. So public needs and tastes, fashion and style, tech interests and uses, as well as manufacturing and mining, all are covered by business journalists.

Business Journalism Lives!

Not surprisingly, even in the midst of wrenching changes in journalism generally, business journalism is thriving. Of the dozens of journalism job openings listed every Friday by Gorkana USA, always half or more are in business journalism, print and online. The employers include Bloomberg, *The Wall Street Journal, American Banker,* metropolitan daily newspapers, city business weeklies like *Crain's Chicago Business* and *South Florida Business Journal,* and specialized industry publications such as Advertising Age, The Deal, Platts, Debtwire, Institutional Investor, Insurance Networking News, Argus Media, and many others. Aggressive online news services such as Quartz and BuzzFeed are expanding their business coverage and thus their business reporting staffs. Less noticed, because their online offerings are by subscription only and cater to highly specialized (and highly demanding!) audiences, are such specialized news services as Reorg Research, in New York, which covers bankruptcy and distressed-business investing, and

Tax Analysts, in suburban Washington, D.C., whose coverage speaks for itself. These business and financial reporting jobs pay better than average, because not all journalists are qualified to handle them.

So why, obscured by the decline of newspaper coverage of all kinds, is business journalism expanding? Why is there a seemingly endless demand for more and better business journalists? Who cares?

Everybody.

Casual readers of online headlines may not see themselves as consumers of business and financial news. But are they seeking a better job? A larger apartment? A deal on a used car? A good rate on a small personal loan? Maybe getting married or raising a family?

Or are they trying to cast an intelligent vote, trying to sort through the promises of the candidates about how they'll improve job opportunities or middle-class pay? Cut taxes? Job training? Tuition assistance? Minimum wage? Crack down on Wall Street fraud?

Are these folks interested in business and financial news? Of course they are. They might not know it, but they are.

Which takes us back to the more traditional consumers of business and financial news, investors and people in business. Even this more refined audience is growing enormously. Half of American families are now invested, directly or indirectly through such vehicles as mutual funds, in the stock market. The near-doubling of working women to 70 million in recent decades has further enlarged the audience for business news.

And let's expand the audience ever further. Think about the movers and shakers of our world, the policy makers, the thought leaders, the public intellectuals, if you will. They used to worry mostly about the Cold War and the Iron Curtain and arms control, but since the 1989–1990 upending of Communist hegemony in Eastern Europe the focus of these thoughtful people is largely economic. Economic development, trade deals, international finance, immigration pressures, monetary policy, exchange rates, and on and on. This is sophisticated stuff. As Finley Peter Dunne might have said, "it ain't beanbag." Who but business journalists can purport to follow this thinking, these policies, and their results—and tell the world what's going on?

The journalists who do this important work—from consumer trends to personal finance to Big Think Economics—are a special breed. Not born, but bred.

These jobs typically require training and sometimes experience in business journalism. So how do you get your foot on the first rung of the ladder? These days, because business and finance are challenging, both to practice and to cover, it's increasingly common that business journalists have some well-focused formal education to prepare and qualify.

Most journalism schools, in both undergraduate and graduate programs, offer a course or two in business journalism, and some even offer master's degrees in business journalism (maybe you're reading this book as part of such a course).

The increasing complexity of business and financial affairs tells us that journalism schools should be training smart, incisive and above all skeptical business reporters. This book is designed to help that process, because credible, effective skepticism must be based on knowledge—knowledge of business and its traditional practices, standards and norms, knowledge of government regulation of business, and, especially, knowledge of how to recognize and call attention to danger. Herein, knowledge. Needless to say, this knowledge, and the skills it facilitates—whether in print, video, Web design or Internet communications—may also be employed in other forms of business or financial communications, for instance, in public relations, investor relations or other corporate communications, government financial communications, even securities analysis.

Because economic and financial understanding, whether imparted through journalism or another profession, always requires numbers, is usually detailed and complex enough to require explanation and interpretation, and demands audience time and attention for optimum comprehension, these stories are best transmitted primarily through text. Yes, they can often be enhanced, supplemented or summarized through audio, still photos, slide shows, video, social media, other websites, and undoubtedly other technological innovations yet to be invented, but until *The Wall Street Journal* and Bloomberg News abandon print there will be a priority need for business journalists to write, and that will be the emphasis in what follows here. As needed, a journalist accomplished in textual communication of the complexities of business, finance and the economy can readily adapt his professional skill to the less comprehensive breezy style of broadcasting, staccato style of Twitter or chunky style of the Internet.

Questions for Discussion

1. How would you define the appropriate scope of business journalism, i.e., where would you draw the outer limits and what subject area(s) would that exclude? Why?
2. Is it justifiable for business publications (and thus, the public) to rely on work by journalists who haven't earned business degrees or actually worked in business or finance? Why or why not?
3. Do you think the business press is influential enough to help the nation avert another catastrophic boom and bust if reporting improves? If so, how?

2 Words

You're embarking into a brave new world. Full of numbers, important and informative numbers, waiting to be discovered, assessed and communicated by you. But to handle them, let's look first at the words, tools at your fingertips to employ usefully and precisely in presenting and characterizing the numbers.

As you familiarize yourself with the words of business journalism, think of your audience. Those men and women know a lot of the terminology of business and investing. But, as you'll see in *The Wall Street Journal* and other well-written business publications, obscure or new terms should be explained, even to them. What's the difference between familiar and new? Understandably, there's no hard and fast rule, but your reading and your own writing will give you a considerable sense of what's standard business language, so when a word or phrase crops up that's unfamiliar, check investopedia.com or ask your instructor, or, if you're still uncertain, err on the side of understanding: include an explanation, and leave it to the editor to decide whether to keep it or strike it.

The Economy

Everyone cares about the economy, at least to some degree, like your own job, for instance. When we refer to the economy, or major aspects of it, certain things come to mind:

Gross domestic product, or GDP: this is the official measure of the economy, meaning the nation's total output of goods and services. **Real GDP**, which means adjusted for inflation, is about $18 trillion in 2016. Two-thirds of our GDP is consumer spending. When times are good, GDP expands. But two consecutive quarters of a contracting GDP, showing a decline in the nation's production of goods and services, translates as **recession** (distinguished from the more ominous **deflation**, which connotes falling prices as well). The **Great Recession** lasted from December 2007 to

June 2009. GDP is measured by the federal Bureau of Economic Analysis, part of the Department of Commerce, which terms its figure an "estimate" and subsequently publishes second and third estimates as it collects and refines more data. **Nominal GDP** is the GDP of a past period as reported in the dollar value of that time, i.e., without adjustment for inflation.

The U.S. **national debt,** ever growing, is often measured against GDP. As of 2016, the debt is about $18 trillion, roughly equal to GDP. This comparison sets off political alarm bells.

A closely watched part of GDP is **industrial production**, which is a measure of the total output of the nation's factories, mines and utilities. Like some other aspects of the economy, industrial production is reported as an index, an artificial construct that, in this case, starts at 2012, or 2012 = 0. Industrial production was 107 in 2015, or 7 percent above 2012, but it's been sliding for several decades in the face of foreign competition, and in 2015 was below its 1972–2014 average.

Closely related to industrial production is **capacity utilization**, showing what percentage of industrial production capabilities are actually in use. It was in the high 70s in 2015, below the 1972–2014 average of 80 percent.

An important aspect of the American economy is real estate activity, and journalists follow various indicators of its health. **Housing starts** is the commencement of construction of both single-family and multi-family homes, measured in numbers of housing units. **New-home sales** are separated from **sales of existing homes,** both reflecting only single-family homes, and both still recovering only fitfully from the Great Recession, which flooded the market with abandoned homes and hordes of others repossessed by mortgage lenders.

An important slice of the economy, one that journalists follow closely, is often called simply **the market**, as in "how's the market?" In fact, it's a number of markets—stocks, bonds, commodities, options, currencies, all sorts of things. But it's the stock market that gets the most attention, and its movement up and down is most often measured by the **Standard & Poor's 500-Stock Index.** (It's the performance benchmark that professional money managers try to beat, and mostly don't.) Other commonly reported measures of the stock market are the **Dow Jones Industrial Average** of just 30 "blue chip" stocks, so-called because, like blue poker chips, they're highly valued, the **NASDAQ Composite Index** (predominantly technology stocks) and the **Russell 2000 Index** (broader than the others, including many smaller companies).

Another closely followed indicator of the economy is the **unemployment rate**. It moved slowly downward in the recovery from the Great Recession, from 10 percent of the workforce in late 2009 to around 5 percent in 2015, a level that's sometimes deemed "full employment" because there's always *frictional unemployment* reflecting the normal movement of people around the country, or from school to job or between jobs or whatever. Note, however, that sometimes the unemployment rate appears to be improving (dropping) when, in fact, it might be because some unemployed workers have become so discouraged that they cease looking for work, i.e., they "drop out" of the workforce. The federal Bureau of Labor Statistics (part of the Department of Labor) says that to be counted as unemployed, a person must be actively seeking work.

While we're getting a grip on "the economy," it's not too soon to define **the Fed**. That's short for the **Federal Reserve Board**, the peculiar name (given partly to obscure its purpose) for the U.S. central bank, located in Washington. It's independent of the government. More likely in recent years, the Fed refers to the **Federal Open Market Committee** comprising the seven members of the Federal Reserve Board and five of the presidents of the 12 regional Federal Reserve Banks that are part of the **Federal Reserve System**. The president of the New York Federal Reserve Bank, by far the largest, is a permanent member of the FOMC; the others rotate in for terms of one year each. The FOMC meets periodically to consider whether it should raise or lower short-term interest rates, a policy decision that's guided by two statutory mandates: to control inflation and to minimize unemployment.

That important interest-rate decision, traditionally implemented by the Fed's deft purchase and sale of U.S. Treasury bonds in the open market, temporarily paled in significance as major financial businesses, overextended in risk, foundered in 2007 and 2008, triggering the financial crisis that became the Great Recession. At that time the Fed, in conjunction with the U.S. Treasury, boldly stepped in and commenced massive monthly purchases of Treasury bonds to inject dollars into the struggling economy. The Fed's purchases were unlimited because it, like other central banks, can "print money" simply by creating bank deposits. This **quantitative easing** is generally credited (along with other government assistance) with resuscitating the economy, preventing the recession from becoming even worse than it was.

The Fed's actions constitute the nation's **monetary policy**, determined, purposefully, by full-time experts, mostly economists, outside the federal government, pretty well insulated from political pressure by the manner of their appointments. The seven members of the Federal Reserve Board are appointed by the U.S. president for terms of 14 years, one term ending in each evenly numbered year, and the presidents of the 12 regional Federal Reserve Banks are elected for five-year terms by each bank's board of directors with the approval of the Federal Reserve Board. The Fed chair is appointed by the president, but his or her 14-year term on the Board usually extends beyond the president's term.

While focusing on the Fed, we must note that it also regulates the nation's largest financial businesses, the **bank holding companies** that own **banks** or **thrift institutions** (both are government-chartered institutions that both accept deposits and make loans, and are themselves separately regulated by state or federal financial agencies) and also conduct huge operations in securities trading and **investment banking** (raising investment capital for businesses). Often, as we'll emphasize later, these bank holding companies or investment banks are erroneously termed "banks" by the press; they're not, but they own most of the country's banks.

Not to be confused with monetary policy is **fiscal policy**, the determination of government revenues and expenditures (and thus the amount of the federal surplus or deficit) each **fiscal year**, by Congress and the president. The nation's fiscal year begins October 1 and ends September 30. (Each state determines its own fiscal year, usually July 1 to June 30.) Congress, at least when it's functioning at its best, actually passes three money bills each year: a **budget authorization**, a guideline which has no force; an **authorization bill** (or cap) for each federal agency; and finally the **appropriation bill** that actually provides the money for each agency to operate.

Watched as closely as GDP and the Fed is the **consumer price index**, or CPI, from the Bureau of Labor Statistics, part of the Department of Labor. This index measures the rise and fall of a "basket" of commonly used goods and services, including food and fuel. If those two big elements are excluded, the remaining figure is called the **Core CPI**. The CPI is generally considered a good indicator of the inflation in the economy, which in turn is a measure of the diminishing purchasing power of the dollar. An alternative, and slower moving, indicator of inflation is the **personal consumption expenditures index**, or **chain-type price index**, calculated by the Bureau of Economic Analysis. Many economists, however, feel that a better measure of inflation is something called the **GDP price deflator**, based on the prices of all goods and services rather than the sometimes-changing select "basket" of goods and services. But the price deflator doesn't get nearly as much attention from business journalists as the consumer-oriented CPI or PCEI.

There are several important measures of consumer well-being, starting with **personal income** and **consumer spending**, both self-explanatory government statistics. Two private surveys of consumers get extensive coverage and, usually, market reaction: the University of Michigan's **Consumer Sentiment Index**, which tracks consumers' personal expectations, and the **Consumer Confidence Index**, from the Conference Board, a New York-based business organization, measuring consumers' attitudes toward the economy in general. These consumer studies make news because consumer spending constitutes two-thirds of the nation's gross domestic product.

However, the other side of this robust consumer activity is that the U.S. **personal savings rate** is very low by international standards, only about 4 percent of disposable income.

Business Organizations

As Robert F. Kennedy found when he ran for president after a lifetime in government, "the business of America is business." As you read about businesses, in news stories, press releases and interviews, you'll encounter various suffixes to company names, important indicators of the legal form of the organization.

Corporations

Most businesses, including all publicly owned companies and nearly all privately owned companies of any size, are incorporated. This is accomplished by filing a fairly simple form with the secretary of state of any state, not to be confused with the United States secretary of state. A corporation is controlled by a board of directors elected by the stockholders. The directors appoint (and can remove) the chief executive officer and other officers of the corporation. Incorporation means that the owners (i.e., the stockholders), the directors and the officers have no *personal* liability for the debts or other obligations of the business. On first reference in your stories, use the full corporate name, with the last word, which is the corporate designation, abbreviated according to Associated Press (AP) style, e.g., Corp., Inc., etc., as detailed below. Also, omit the comma before a final Inc. or Ltd. and omit the initial word "The," even if these depart from the company's legal name. AP style rules.

A corporation is indicated by

> Inc. (Incorporated)
> Corp. (Corporation)
> Ltd. (Limited)
> PLC (public liability company, mostly U.K. companies)
> SA (French or Italian share company)
> GmbH (German)
> NV (Dutch)
> *etc.*

If you're not sure about a public company's name, check the cover page of any of its filings with the Securities and Exchange Commission (sec.gov) (Forms10K, 10Q, etc.). More on these documents later.

If the company has no public stockholders, that means it's privately held. There are innumerable private companies in the U.S., most of them tiny but including some of the largest, such as grains giant Cargill Inc. To find out the proper legal name of a private corporation (as well as a public corporation), search the secretary of state's website of the state where the company is incorporated. For instance, in Illinois you'd view the Illinois Secretary of State's list of businesses that hold a current Certificate of Good Standing authorizing them to do business in the state: www.cyberdriveillinois.com. Most businesses are incorporated in the state where the headquarters is located, but another possibility is Delaware, whose law is friendly to corporations and where many large businesses located elsewhere are incorporated. Corporate information is available from the Secretary of State's Division of Corporations: http://corp.delaware.gov/index.shtml. However, there's a charge for a search.

Professional Corporation (PC)

This corporate form is used by doctors, lawyers and other professionals to limit their personal liability; a PC can be just one person or a firm.

Limited Liability Company (LLC)

This form requires less record keeping and paperwork than a corporation, but offers the owners limited liability and some tax advantages.

Unincorporated Businesses

Some businesses operate without incorporating, meaning the owners retain full personal liability for debts, lawsuits and other obligations of the business.

Sole Proprietorship

This business has a single owner.

Partnership

This usually means a *general* partnership, in which each partner is *fully* liable personally for *all* obligations of the business, not just one-half or one-third. But there's also a *limited* partnership (LP), which is a vehicle used by some capital-hungry businesses, notably oil and gas exploration companies.

14 *Words*

They have *general* **partners**, who run the business and are personally liable for its obligations, and *limited* **partners**, outside investors who have no management role and no personal liability beyond the risk of their own investments in the business. In both general and limited partnerships, the partnership is not taxed; all profits flow through to the partners, who are taxed personally on their income.

Do we need to explore and explain all this in writing about these various kinds of businesses? No. Readers of business stories understand such background, but it is important that we provide the full name, with the Inc. or LP or whatever, and know what it means.

Sources for Business Stories

Business stories require perspective, interpretation, maybe even analysis. It doesn't do the reader much good to know that a company made a million dollars unless we compare that against previous earnings, and state what the securities analysts covering the company expected it to earn. But it's not your job to originate the information needed for perspective and interpretation. That's what the analysts do—and economists, and business consultants, and data gatherers, and other experts.

Securities Analysts

Equity analysts study and analyze the stocks and estimate the future earnings of publicly held companies. They usually specialize in a particular industry, e.g., retailing or banking or transportation. Most analysts work for securities firms that also do investment banking and retail stock brokerage. Chicago-based Morningstar Inc., a large company that's publicly held itself, is a notable exception; it does research only, and so do some small firms. Some analysts specialize in fixed-income securities (bonds) issued by public companies. These **fixed-income analysts**, such as Gimme Credit LLC, monitor whether the company can meet its debt obligations, both principal and interest; they don't estimate earnings or rate stocks or set target prices. However, they can be sources to fall back on for an earnings story if you can't reach the equity analysts who cover the company.

Asset Managers (Portfolio Managers)

They buy and sell publicly held securities on behalf of mutual funds, pension funds, endowment funds and other large **institutional investors**. They're usually the biggest holders of a public company's securities.

Economists

They're in universities and large companies, notably commercial banks and investment banks. Others work for large business associations such as the National Association of Manufacturers (NAM). Some economists specialize in a certain aspect of the economy, e.g., labor or international trade.

Consultants

They provide expert services and advice to companies in a particular industry, e.g., manufacturing or software or telecommunications, and sometimes conduct surveys or studies of the industry and its customers, which may be the general public. Some are university faculty.

Professors

Whether they consult or not, experts on everything; search www.profnet.com for both professors and consultants, or write your own search terms on the site. Most university PR offices will be happy to refer you to a professor who's expert in your topic (a good way to localize a national story).

Trade Publication Editors and Reporters

They work for magazines or Web publications or newsletters that cover a certain industry, e.g., farm equipment or pharmaceuticals. They know the companies, the trends, the problems and the outlook for that industry. You may quote them as sources, and it's OK to borrow a story *idea* from a trade pub, but of course do your own reporting.

Trade and Professional Associations

They may be national, like the National Retail Merchants Association, the Pharmaceutical Research and Manufacturers of America, and the American Medical Association, or they may be similar state organizations, such as the Illinois Retail Merchants Association. They sometimes conduct studies or surveys useful to their members (and to the press). They usually have good PR people who know their industry and its major players, and may be able to recommend sources, though they don't comment on individual companies. (Let's note here that PR people, like lawyers and securities analysts and virtually everyone in the economy, have a personal economic interest, maybe even an ax to grind; the journalistic antidote is to use multiple sources to the extent possible.)

Troubled (and Troubling) Securities

At the bottom of the Great Recession of 2007–2009, and the very slow recovery that followed, were **subprime mortgage loans**, home loans made on extremely easy terms by mortgage brokers or bank loan officers to buyers who were counting on an unending appreciation of real estate values. These buyers could not qualify for traditional home loans, generally characterized by a down payment of 20 percent or 30 percent, monthly payments (the total of debt service, real estate taxes and insurance) of no more than 30 percent of their gross income, and monthly reduction of the total amount of the loan (amortization) over 20 or 30 years, to zero.

Casting aside these traditional standards of prudent mortgage lending, bankers and brokers eager to collect fees made the loans anyway, often requiring no money down and monthly payments of interest only (or even less than that, which meant the loans actually *increased* over time). The originators of these flimsy loans then sold them to an investment bank or to the big government-chartered mortgage companies, Freddie Mac and Fannie Mae, which used them as backing (collateral) for bonds, described below, that they sold to investors. The serious breaches of prudent standards by the mortgage lenders led to a cascade of default.

Mortgage-Backed Securities (MBS)

An MBS is a bond created and sold by an investment bank or the government-chartered mortgage companies, secured (collateralized) by an interest in a large pool of home mortgage loans. Many of these mortgages, in the run-up to the crisis, were the risky **subprime** loans. Nevertheless, rating agencies such as Standard & Poor's and Moody's Investors Services often rated these MBS bonds as triple-A, the safest, on the untested notion that the equity in the hundreds or thousands of homes subject to those mortgages would surely be sufficient to cover any losses should the issuer of the MBS prove unable to honor its commitments to pay interest and principal to the investors who bought the bonds. Not so, as it turned out.

Collateralized Debt Obligations (CDO)

A CDO is a bond secured by, guess what, a large pool of mortgage-backed securities. CDOs, too, obtained triple-A ratings from the rating agencies without verification of the ultimate value of the collateral in the event of default.

Credit Default Swaps (CDS)

This is an insurance-type commitment by a company (e.g., American International Group) promising to pay the holder (owner) of a bond (e.g., an MBS or CDO) if the security is defaulted. These "insurance policies" were negotiable, and the ensuing speculative trading in CDSs proved disastrous in the Great Recession. The CDS trading in turn triggered speculation in the bonds they backed, in effect speculating on whether the bonds (and perhaps the companies behind them) were worth their stated value. In the end many weren't, leading to mass defaults by the CDS issuers (the insurers) who couldn't meet their commitments. The government bailed out AIG.

Asset-Backed Commercial Paper

This is a very short-term obligation (measured in days) of a company that sold the paper to raise temporary operating cash, backed (collateralized) by other securities (e.g., MBS or CDO) in order to obtain a lower rate in the market. (Traditionally, commercial paper was issued only by companies with such strong finances that the paper required *no collateralization*, so the name "asset-backed commercial paper" was itself an intentionally misleading label that the press should have flagged.)

Banks, municipalities and government agencies are still reeling under the weight of defaulted and frequently abandoned homes that were the hallmarks of the Great Recession. It's important today to know this history of yesterday because it's still with us, and the above terms are essential to that understanding.

Useful Verbs of Attribution

We are blessed with a beautifully expressive language, English. It permits us to express shades of precise meaning. Nuances and coloration are always possible. So, even in the business world, for all its inescapable facts and abundant numbers, it's appropriate to take advantage of the language when attributing quotes (contrary to some teaching that only "said" or "stated" are acceptable). This is especially true when our sources make statements of varying validity and credibility. They may, on the one hand, simply take note of established, known facts, or, on the other hand, express claims or allegations that sound dubious and which you can't verify, at least not on deadline. Good journalism allows for use of such questionable statements (how could reporters cover *politics* without quoting them?), for they can serve to enhance your story. However, they can be characterized as questionable or unproven by the verbs you use to present them.

18 Words

Here are three lists of useful verbs of attribution, categorized on the left as references to known facts or truths, on the right as contentious or arguable, and down the middle, neutral or straightforward, without innuendo:

Referencing Established Fact	Neutral	Contentious
pointed out	said	alleged
noted	stated	asserted
observed	announced	averred
emphasized	iterated	commented
underscored	disclosed	claimed
referenced	reiterated	opined
	continued	argued
	went on	insisted
	remarked	postulated
	explained	expostulated
	added	suggested
	read	countered
	declared	prophesied
	presented	predicted
	unveiled	barked
	published	whispered
		objected
		contended
		proposed
		demanded
		worried
		offered
		exulted

A word of caution: the verb "explained" is not a synonym for "said" or "stated." It's used, not surprisingly, only to attribute an *explanation*.

Glitches

Before we leave words, let's look at a few common misuses of them in business writing.

Adjusted earnings as an adequate substitute for *profit* or *net income*: while net income (or profit) is defined by Generally Accepted Accounting Principles, and is required by the Securities and Exchange Commission, adjusted earnings are not standard; they are simply a company's inflated distortion of its actual earnings, typically created by omitting significant expenses or charges.

Compared *to* instead of compared *with* (and sometimes the reverse): the former is used to demonstrate a contrast between two dissimilar facts or numbers, the latter to compare two similar items, like this year's net income vs. last year's.

Percent instead of *percentage points*: use percent change to state the difference between two numbers (9 is 90 percent of 10), and percentage points to state the change or difference between two percents (15 percent is five percentage points greater than 10 percent).

Report or news occurred *today;* unless your organization prescribes *today,* either state the day, or omit reference to a day.

Spinoff as a synonym for a sale or divestiture or initial public offering: spinoff means only the splitting off a portion of a company as a new, separate company, with its shares simply given, proportionately and without charge, to the shareholders of the original company. (These transactions are tax-free, which encourages them.)

Secondary offering used incorrectly to describe a public offering of securities by a company at any time after its Initial Public Offering: it is in fact an offering of securities by the *individual owners* of those securities (usually the company's founders or early investors) rather than by the company, meaning that the company obtains no benefit from the offering, all proceeds accruing only to the selling shareholders.

Bank referring to a bank holding company or an investment company rather than a commercial bank: a bank holding company, most commonly an investment bank such as JP Morgan Chase & Co. or Citigroup Inc., owns a commercial bank (or an S&L) as well as other financial subsidiaries such as a securities broker or an insurance company. It's OK to call the bank holding company a *banking company*. But the word *bank* properly means a commercial bank, which is a government-chartered institution that both accepts deposits and makes loans. More on banks later.

Bankrupt, referring to an individual or a company that's filed in U.S. Bankruptcy Court for protection from creditors under the Bankruptcy Act: such a person or company isn't necessarily bankrupt. The word doesn't have any reference to a bankruptcy filing; it means that the debtor's liabilities exceed its assets or that the debtor can't pay its obligations as they come due. More on bankruptcy later, too.

More generally, it's unacceptable to use a term or a phrase from a press release or interview without understanding it and without explanation (e.g., "a deemed dividend" is not a standard term, so must be explained or defined if it's to be used). When uncertain whether the usage is standard or calls for explanation, check investopedia.com or ask your instructor, as noted above. If still in doubt, explain.

As you've seen, the vocabulary of business is not bizarre or peculiar. It may call for use of some words that you don't use in everyday conversation or other writing, but they're standard English with standard meanings. They're not jargon or "street talk." And when you become familiar with their meaning and their usage, you've acquired an expressive advantage that gives meaning to the words "business writing." Remember, it's a marketable skill.

Questions for Discussion

1 What other words can you think of that journalists (or other smart people) use in describing something about business or the economy, and what do those words mean to you? How can you find out for sure?
2 Why do the *contentious* verbs of attribution so greatly outnumber the straightforward, indisputable verbs?
3 Give an example of how a mistaken use of *percent* will distort a comparison that should be stated as *percentage points*. Hint: don't compare a particular percent (such as the unemployment rate) with another by percent difference or percent change.
4 In *The Wall Street Journal* or another business publication, find a word or expression that's new to you, to see whether it's explained or not; make your own assessment as to whether that represents good business writing.

3 Numbers

In all journalism, not just business and finance, numbers impart specificity, firmness and credibility. Thus a wide variety of news stories employ numbers to make their point. In business journalism, of course, numbers often are the backbone of the story. It's clearly impossible to tell the tale of Americans' living and working without noting essentials of their lives such as income, spending, prices paid, saving and investing. Stories about government—appropriations, taxes, budgets, spending on weapons and social services, everything—can hardly be told without numbers.

It's important to recognize that, when you come to writing about the economy, or the markets, or some other broad-brush treatment of the financial facts of life, you first need to comprehend the elements, the constituent parts, that comprise the economy or some other broad aspect of it. A simple example: if you're writing about the sum total of corporate profits in a certain quarter or a certain year, you clearly need to understand what the individual corporate profits are that make up that total. Or, to cover the government's release of gross domestic product, the GDP, you need to know that it's the total output of the nation's goods and services, and to know how they're measured.

So, to start building that base of understanding, you'll want to know that in business journalism, THE most basic story is about the quarterly financial reports required by our securities laws of all companies that are publicly held, i.e., whose shares are traded on the stock market. To write that story, let's do the numbers.

Read the Financial Statement

At the end of each fiscal quarter (usually the calendar quarter, but not necessarily), a public company must publish a financial statement of its revenues (or sales) and profits (or earnings), its assets, such as equipment and real estate, and its liabilities, such as debts owed to its banks and its bondholders.

22 *Numbers*

This financial statement generally is accompanied by a press release calling attention to the most favorable numbers in the statement, or sometimes making up numbers that don't belong in the financial statement, augmented by self-congratulatory quotations attributed to the head of the company, its chief executive officer, or CEO, or perhaps the chief financial officer, the CFO. No matter what the press release says, you must consult the financial statements.

The Most Vital Numbers

The first priorities to spot are, at the top of the **statement of operations, revenues** (**sales** are the numerical equivalent, but "revenues" may include interest revenue or fees or other receipts that aren't exactly "sales"; use whichever term the company uses, and don't say the company "earned" revenue, quite confusing), and then at the bottom, **net income** (the same as **earnings** or **profit**) or net loss, both the total number and then expressed as **per share of common stock** outstanding (shares in the hands of shareholders). Ergo, a reference to "top line" means revenues, and "bottom line" means net income. The statement also sets forth the comparative figures for a year earlier. These numbers, and all others in the statement (if not the press release), are defined by the accounting profession's **Generally Accepted Accounting Principles**, or GAAP. Thus, "GAAP net income."

A growing or improving company is reflected, logically enough, in rising revenues. If revenues rise and the company controls its expenses for wages, materials, rent and other necessary costs of doing business, its net income (that's the proper accounting term, though earnings or profit are synonyms and may be used interchangeably) will rise, too. If revenues rise but net income doesn't, look for excesses in the **operating expenses**, such as cost of materials and advertising expense.

Let's examine, for instance, the first quarter 2014 report of GrubHub Inc., a newly public, fast-growing, Chicago-based company that handles online food orders and deliveries. Both revenues and net income leapt in that quarter: revenues to $56,613,000 (figures presented are in thousands, which means you add three 0s) from $39,377,000 (the "pro forma" total including an acquired New York company prior to its acquisition in August 2013), **net income attributable to common stockholders** (the full, proper accounting term) to $4,353,000 from $659,000. These net income figures are also divided by the number of common shares outstanding (again, owned by investors) and stated as **net income per share**, which is a key investment metric: 8 cents per basic share (based on the actual number of shares outstanding) in the 2014 quarter versus 1 cent per basic share a year earlier. However, if you add in all the shares that the company is obligated to issue in the future, mainly through executives' **stock-option** compensation (company commitments to issue shares to these executives in the future at lower prices based on earlier market levels), then the **net income *per diluted share*** is reduced to 6 cents (from 8 cents) versus a year-earlier 1 cent. Because the **diluted** figures are lower, more conservative, they are emphasized by both securities analysts and business journalists; the **diluted** adjective must be stated in your story. Here are the statements published by the company:

GRUBHUB, INC.

	Three Months Ended March 31, 2014	Three Months Ended March 31, 2013 Pro Forma Combined
	(in thousands)	
Revenues	58,613	39,377
Costs and expenses	58,13	
Sales and marketing	16,117	14,946
Operations and support	15,107	10,687
Technology (exclusive of amortization)	5,347	4,307
General and administrative	8,324	5,559
Depreciation and amortization	5,515	2,414
Total operating expenses	50,410	37,913
Income before provision for income taxes	8,203	1,464
Provision for income taxes	3,850	805
Net income attributable to common stockholders	4,353	659
Net income per share attributable to common stockholders:		
Basic	0.08	0.01
Diluted	0.06	0.01

(continued)

24 Numbers

GRUBHUB, INC. (*continued*)

	Three Months Ended March 31, 2014	Three Months Ended March 31, 2013 Pro Forma Combined
	(in thousands)	
Weighted average number of shares outstanding:		
Basic	55,210	54,682
Diluted	77,635	74,563

KEY PRO FORMA OPERATING METRICS

	Three Months Ended March 31,	
	2014	2013 Pro Forma
Active Diners (000s)	3,851	2,577
Daily Average Grubs	181,200	129,100
Gross Food Sales (millions)	433	300

Other numbers helpful in assessing the company's performance may be found on the company's **balance sheet**, its statement of assets and liabilities at the end of the quarter (with a comparison with a year earlier): check for rising or falling debt, changes in investment in productive assets like buildings and machinery, and increases or decreases in **stockholders' equity**, which is the value of the company according to accounting rules (as distinct from the market value of the company's shares, called **market capitalization**). In GrubHub's case, while its total assets at March 31, 2014, were greater than a year earlier, so were its total liabilities (both **short-term** liabilities, which are obligations due within one year, and **long-term** liabilities, the total of all other obligations), with the result that stockholders' equity, even as the business was growing, actually declined a bit, to $548,203,000 from $557,375,000. Worth noting, but not significant enough to write about in this case.

GRUBHUB INC.
CONDENSED CONSOLIDATED BALANCE SHEETS - UNAUDITED

(in thousands, except share data)

ASSETS	March 31, 2014	December 31, 2013
CURRENT ASSETS:		
Cash and cash equivalents	$112,760	$86,542
Accounts receivable	38,116	27,725
Income taxes receivable	1,821	1,579
Deferred taxes, current	3,688	3,688
Prepaid expenses	2,352	2,625
Total current assets	158,737	122,159
PROPERTY AND EQUIPMENT:		
Property and equipment, net of depreciation and amortization	17,332	17,096
OTHER ASSETS:		
Other assets	1,975	2,328
Goodwill	352,788	352,788
Acquired intangible assets, net of amortization	264,915	268,441
Total other assets	619,678	623,557
TOTAL ASSETS	$795,747	$762,812
LIABILITIES, REDEEMABLE COMMON STOCK AND STOCKHOLDERS' EQUITY		
CURRENT LIABILITIES:		
Accounts payable	$3,297	$3,353
Restaurant food liability	96,923	78,245

(continued)

GRUBHUB INC.
CONDENSED CONSOLIDATED BALANCE SHEETS - UNAUDITED
(continued)

(in thousands, except share data)

CURRENT LIABILITIES:	March 31, 2014	December 31, 2013
Taxes payable	1,046	1,768
Accrued payroll	2,663	1,720
Other accruals	11,085	7,505
Total current liabilities	115,014	92,591
LONG TERM LIABILITIES:		
Deferred taxes, non-current	94,805	90,495
Other accruals	2,775	3,936
Total long term liabilities	97,580	94,431
Redeemable common stock	34,950	18,415
STOCKHOLDERS' EQUITY:		
Series A Convertible Preferred Stock	2	2
Common stock	5	5
Accumulated other comprehensive income	181	132
Additional paid-in capital	486,782	500,356
Retained earnings	61,233	56,880
Total Stockholders' Equity	$548,203	$557,375
TOTAL LIABILITIES AND STOCKHOLDERS' EQUITY	$795,747	$762,812

Other Numbers May Be Useful

The ratio of the company's debt to its shareholders' equity (debt-to-equity ratio), its depreciation (the year-by-year diminution in value of machinery, buildings and other assets, deducted from earnings), cash flow (profit plus depreciation, set forth in another of the required financial statements) and other numbers may be significant, especially if a company is encountering choppy waters. When you interview securities analysts for their comments on a company financial report, they may call attention to some of these less obvious numbers.

Goodwill and Impairment

In the modern era of incessant acquisitions of one company by another, sometimes called mergers, the accounting terms **goodwill** and **impairment** have assumed great significance in the financial results of an acquiring company. The acquirer, let's call it company A, often pays more (in cash or common stock, or a combination of the two) for a target company (company T) than the amount of T's stockholders' equity on its balance sheet. The excess is called goodwill, and accounting rules require that it be recorded (or booked) on A's balance sheet as an asset. In the case of GrubHub, which had acquired another company, Seamless Holdings, in 2013, the goodwill asset, both at March 31, 2014 and a year earlier, is stated as $352,788,000. If it turns out later, as it often does, that the performance of T, now called a **subsidiary**, is less than expected, so T itself is worth less than A paid, accounting rules require that the goodwill be appraised and reduced or even eliminated from the balance sheet of A. This reduction is called an impairment, and that dollar amount must simultaneously be deducted from A's earnings for the quarter, even though its actual cash income is unaffected. Sometimes an impairment can have an immense negative impact on A's earnings, even turning a profit into a loss. If so, the company will surely point that out. But watch for impairments, common these days, sometimes with major consequences for the operating statement. If so, your story should point that out.

Read the Press Release, Skeptically

Bear in mind that the press release, like all others, is not objective or disinterested. It's designed to put the best possible face on the financial statement, to call your attention to the numbers most favorable to the company. It will play down, sometimes even ignore, embarrassing numbers, particular if they're the "bottom line," the company's net income or profit for the quarter. For instance, if the press release leads with a focus on sales, or some non-standard (non-GAAP) representation of performance such as "adjusted earnings" or "earnings before one-time charges" (both of which the company will define in any way it wants), it may be because the actual earnings aren't so hot.

28 *Numbers*

Useful Explanations

Explanations such as an impairment or other unusual deductions from earnings will typically be set forth, probably emphasized, in the press release. Such notations can be helpful, as can breakdowns of numbers that go beyond the requirements of the financial statement: for instance, sales in Asia, Europe and other continents separated from North American sales. Comparing them with year-earlier figures may help shine a light on why, and where, the company did better or worse than a year ago, and that's a useful aspect of your story.

Dissimulation?

As we said, the company's main purpose in the press release, particularly if the quarter was disappointing, is to put a gloss on the results. However, the numbers in the *financial statements* are governed by accounting rules (GAAP) and the Securities and Exchange Commission, which regulates stock trading and the disclosure of information by the companies whose stocks are publicly traded. Therefore your reliance is best placed on the figures in the financial statements rather than those in the press release. In fact, if in its press release the company wants to create and call your attention to non-GAAP "earnings" figures like those mentioned above, they won't appear in the financial statement at all, because they're unofficial. That's not to say that securities analysts and investors will have no interest in such conjurations, so perhaps you'll want to mention them in your earnings story, particularly if analysts focus on them, but GAAP earnings are always your first priority.

One common diversion is EBITDA, short for **Earnings Before Interest, Taxes, Depreciation and Amortization**. With such big omissions on the expense side, the bottom line is inevitably going to be higher than real GAAP earnings. Depreciation and amortization are proper accounting terms, expressing the declining value of property and equipment, and of certain financial obligations, on each year's balance sheet, declines that must also be reflected in reductions (by the same amounts) of net income on the statement of operations, though there's no reduction in actual cash income.

Even more slippery, companies may crow about their **adjusted earnings**, which omit major expenses and have no accepted definition at all; in other words, the company defines the number any way it wants. It's absolutely phony.

To emphasize: in any deviation from GAAP net income, all the expense exclusions are completely at the discretion of the company. There's no standardization that would permit an objective comparison of one company's results with another, or even quarter-to-quarter comparisons of the same company's results.

Your best rule: read the press release critically and skeptically; look for corroboration (or lack thereof) in the financial statement. And don't be misled by analysts' rosy attention to non-GAAP "earnings." Remember, with few exceptions, analysts on are Wall Street's "sell" side. Their intention is to stimulate interest in stocks. More on deceptions in coming chapters.

Quotations

As mentioned above, the press release probably will contain a comment from the chief executive officer (CEO) or chief financial officer (CFO) about the quarter's performance. If they're helpful to your explanation of why the quarter was up or down, it's OK to use such quotes, properly attributed to "a press release" or "a statement." But skip over self-serving congratulations such as "we had a great quarter." If the press release and the financial statements raise questions in your mind or require further explanation, call the company's public relations office (or investor relations), or, if they can't answer your questions, call the company CFO or treasurer. Just ask for a "layman's explanation" of the number or term that puzzles you. If you obtain such a quote, attribute it to "an interview."

Expert Interpretation

We don't need to interpret the significance of the numbers ourselves. For that we turn to the experts, especially the securities analysts who follow and continuously assess the company's stock for investment companies like Bank of America Merrill Lynch, Morgan Stanley, BMO Capital Markets, Raymond James, William Blair & Company, A.G. Edwards, Edward Jones, Stifel Nicolaus and Robert W. Baird & Co., or for securities research firms like Morningstar Inc. Some publicly held companies will list on their websites the names of the analysts who follow them.

Other possible sources of explanatory or interpretive quotes are asset managers—managers of pension funds, mutual funds, college endowments and other large money pools—who have invested clients' money in the stock.

Analysts' Expectations

Before writing your earnings story, check a financial data site like Yahoo Finance or Zacks Investment Research to get the securities analysts' consensus earnings-per-share estimate (forecast) for the relevant quarter.

In your earnings story you'll need to compare that expectation with the actual earnings. At finance.yahoo.com, for instance, we learn that the consensus first-quarter estimate of the analysts was that GrubHub would earn 3 cents per share (and we can assume that's per *diluted* share). The earnings story is a challenge, and this is but a start. However, it's the essential key to understanding business as well as to writing about it. If you find all this new terminology difficult to digest at first, bear with us, for we'll be using the words over and over again, and you'll soon find them quite familiar—and very useful!

Questions for Discussion

1 Does it matter whether a publicly held company makes money? Why? Is the answer the same for a privately owned company? Why or why not?
2 How do you account for the difference between *basic* earnings per share and *diluted* earnings per share? Which is the best representation of a company's actual results? Which do securities analysts and journalists use? Why? Does this seem reasonable to you?
3 Devise a mnemonic to help remind you of the difference between **revenue (sales)** and **net income (earnings, profit)**. They *must* not be confused.
4 If a company emphasizes "adjusted earnings" in its press release, and securities analysts also refer to that number, does it have some value for your story? Then what about GAAP net income (which must appear in the financial statement)? More on this ahead.

4 People

At bottom, it's about people, isn't it?

That's what makes business journalism vital, even important. It affects people's lives. It may be powerful, poignant or perplexing. It may be comforting, confounding or even cataclysmic (but never, if it's done well, confusing or condescending).

So, amidst all the numbers, how do we ensure that we keep people in our hearts?

Happily, this motivational imperative coincides with a journalistic imperative: get quotes into every business story. They may be illustrative, they may be professionally interpretive, they may be questionable advocacy or spin, they may be quite personal, they may even be irrational, but talk to people and get at least some of their words into your story, every story. So let's look at several types of people you might interview and how they might fit into your stories.

Corporate Officers

Publicly Held Companies

Yes, they have big titles and big responsibilities, but they're people, too. For, while they speak on behalf of their companies, in fact they're representing themselves at the same time, because part of the challenge of their big jobs is to present themselves favorably, too.

Prepare well for such an interview, even if it's likely to be brief. Realistically, you're not likely to schedule a personal interview with the CEO or CFO of a big company, but they might pick up your phone call, or, better yet, pursue them immediately after a shareholders meeting, a ribbon-cutting, a speech or other public event. When you're on deadline and need a quick explanation or comment on a financial matter, try the company's treasurer. The treasurer isn't a policy maker but definitely knows the numbers and probably isn't deluged with press calls.

If you're questioning the CEO or CFO, do your homework especially carefully. Learn who the executive is, something about his or her background, and what's been published recently about the person and about the company. How's the stock doing? Has the executive been quoted recently by a newspaper or network or news service? High-level execs don't suffer fools gladly. Take full advantage of whatever minutes (or moments) you may grab with them.

Know exactly what you'll ask. It may be helpful to rehearse a lead question or two in your mind, with the words you intend to use. If you want to follow up on something the person was quoted as saying, even in a company press release, offer a quick reminder of what that was and where you saw it.

Don't be afraid to challenge or question something the exec said, either previously or in your own interview. You'll want to be respectful and polite (they're used to being treated respectfully and politely), but that doesn't mean you have to accept everything he or she says at face value, particularly if other authoritative voices, say, securities analysts or government officials, have already expressed their own questions or doubts on that subject.

In a face-to-face situation, once you've got your questions answered, extract your phone and ask the exec if it's OK to take a picture. Your default position may be to use the exec's photo on the company's website, but that genre is stilted and looks inappropriate to illustrate an interview.

If, after your interview, you have any doubt about what the exec said or the words you intend to quote, run it by the company's public affairs or PR office. Describe where and how you got the quote, and give them an opportunity to object to your wording. This doesn't mean you're offering the right to deny or veto your story or your quote. Hold your ground if you're confronted by such a riposte and you're confident of your story, even if you remain uncertain about the exact words. Just do your best to quote them accurately.

Apart from quoting the exec in what presumably will be a spot news story, could you reuse those same words, or others from your interview, in a more subjective, longer piece, perhaps about the company's management or a personal profile of the person? This would be a considerably more challenging story, not likely within the ambit of a junior journalist. Leave that one to your editor or a senior reporter.

And about that speech by a top exec: don't take it at face value. If it's an appearance before a business organization or other public gathering, look for what's new, about the company or the economy or even about the executive personally, and don't be distracted by blarney or bluster. Your news standard remains the same despite what may be an august setting. Then, after the speech, get some audience reaction. Ask a few people what they learned, what they'll take away—beyond the fact that this prominent person was at the dais. If you conclude that the speech and the reaction were uniformly ho-hum, so be it. Don't report anything.

Private Companies

You'll find much more opportunity here, for video and still photos as well as text. In fact, whether your objective is a personal profile or a story about the business (or some other angle, like a business trend piece), your story (or segment) can probably be constructed around pictures of the boss. This isn't a distortion of news judgment. In any small business, the boss IS the story. More on that type of story later.

In the meantime, focus on the person—literally as well as figuratively.

Still Photos

A still photo can make even a dull subject (let's face it: some business people are) eye-catching, even a bit dramatic. But a good one takes some planning, and some time to execute. And don't treat the photo shoot as an afterthought following an interview. Give it priority, up front, while both you and the boss are fresh to the task

Following are some very practical, very professional, tips, based on advice and counsel generously given to Medill School business classes by Steve Liss, talented and imaginative former *Time/Life* photographer, former instructor at the Medill School, now at Columbia College in Chicago.

First, arrange to arrive at your photo location, presumably the company's premises, 15 or 20 minutes before your appointment with the boss. Take time to look around and find possible photo locations or backgrounds with adequate natural light. It can be soft or indirect, maybe from the side, creating facial shadows. A shop or factory floor can appear enticing, but a predominance of artificial light may be a problem there. At the same time, offices are tough: usually sterile, boring. If that's your only option, be certain you're not shooting toward an open window. But try to get the boss out of the office. Where? Exteriors, courtyards, reception areas, even hallways, perhaps a spot where you can position your camera above or below your subject (a stairway, a balcony, a garden) to get a different angle, looking up or down. An unconventional location may justify, even enhance, an obviously posed photo, e.g., a straight-into-the-camera gaze. But the informality of an over-the-shoulder shot of a conversation with a colleague can be equally engaging.

34 People

If you must settle for a photo at the desk, talk to your subject as you work your camera (better a DSLR here) in a close-up position. With continuous chatter, instruct him or her to turn or talk or laugh or gesture or look up or down or pick up the phone or put it down, all the while shooting rapidly, capturing a variety of motions and expressions.

Try to observe the "rule of thirds," placing your subject in the right or left third of your frame rather than in the middle, and his or her head in the middle horizontal third. (If you flub, of course, you may be able to achieve this by cropping.)

Thank you, Steve.

Video

Think in advance how you want your video to play in your story. Is it the whole story, self-standing? Or will it enhance a text? Visualize your end product. For instance, you won't want to cut a video interview with the same quotes you're using in your text. What other possibilities are there?

Outdoors is better. Avoid backlight. Get a mix of wide shots (an "establisher"), medium shots and close-ups, shoot far more B-roll (with ambient sound, if it's available) than you think you'll need to cover your audio, and mike all your speaking subjects. Quality sound is vital, and too easily overlooked as you concentrate on the substance of your story idea and the quality of your video. Indistinct or off-mike or otherwise inadequate voice can scuttle a perfectly good picture or interview. Record your voice-over later in a studio or other closed space. To avoid any resemblance to screeching TV commercials, do not resort to their editing techniques of jump cuts and one-second scenes—so easy to cut, so jarring to watch.

Other People

Many business stories, including those based on data, can be enhanced by interviewing people at random on the street, be they consumers or taxpayers or transit riders or even visitors from out-of-town (in the right locations, of course). The purpose is to elicit personal views, personal observations, personal experiences, not to collect amateur opinions of the data. For instance, if your story is about consumer prices moving up or down, you might ask people whether they're noticing price changes and whether it affects their shopping in any way. You need not interview a lot of people, trying to justify a claim that you've done a public opinion poll, for your story emphasizes data. Your interviews are illustrative, not authoritative. Just refer to your responses as an opinion sample or random interviews rather than a poll. Of course you'll want to query enough people to get a variety of answers.

These random interviews can be strictly old style, pencil and paper, or they can be video or audio, depending on your needs. Even if your product will be text-only, you may want to record audio to quote more accurately, but most states stipulate that any recording of a conversation may be done only with the consent of both parties, so show your subject your recording device and give him or her a chance to object. With or without audio, get the person's name and age, and probably, depending on the nature of your questioning, residence and job as well.

If you want video, you'll need a partner to operate the camera while you conduct the interviews (or perhaps trade off). Shoot only one-shots, excluding yourself from the picture. Try to use different views, with different backgrounds, for your different interviews, so that your edited result doesn't show a ridiculous succession of talking heads popping in and out of the same scene.

Look for other ways to introduce people into business stories, i.e., to humanize them. Sometimes government activity or reports will help point the way. For instance, Illinois law requires employers to give 60 days' advance notice when they intend to lay off 25 or more workers if the number constitutes one-third or more of the company's total workforce. These notices, though not announced, are publicly available. They give an alert journalist an opportunity to interview both the company and the employees likely to be affected. A statistic becomes a very human news story. Similarly, jobless persons filing claims for unemployment benefits may be seen entering and leaving state employment offices. You shouldn't try to interview or photograph them in the office, but you can try on the street.

Labor union actions, particularly picket lines, provide excellent opportunities to see the human side of business news, but it's important to interview individual marchers, not just their union leaders, articulate and forceful though they may be. The focus of the story is the workers. Though union strikes are dwindling these days, unions sometimes foment other newsworthy worker activity, such as the recurrent demonstrations by fast-food employees seeking a $15 minimum hourly wage. (For once, video is the best way to cover a real business story.)

Despite these occasional, accessible, visual opportunities to highlight people in the economy, let's face it, most of us work in offices, don't walk picket lines, and come and go quite inconspicuously. So journalists can't just wait for some sort of disruptive event to cover the vast human side of economic activity. One answer is to seek out and propound stories about work, about money, about consumers, stories that are built around "people." We'll explore this kind of story later.

Questions for Discussion

1 Would it be responsible, credible journalism to seek out "people" for your stories on the Internet? How might you satisfy yourself, and your audience?
2 If you interview a person who's helpful but inarticulate, or doesn't enunciate clearly, can you still use that person in your story? How?
3 How would you define the difference between a person who has some significance in a broader story and a person whose news value is merely "human interest"?

5 The Earnings Story

There's no way to get comfortable with writing earnings stories (and, for that matter, any business stories dealing with financial matters) except by writing them—quite a few of them. But, once mastered, the earnings story will be your gateway to the entire world of business and finance, consumers' as well as companies'. So let's get on with it.

There's more than one way to write the earnings story, but the format recommended here is comprehensive, and learning it can serve as a springboard for writing more interpretive earnings stories in the future, if that's appropriate for your publication.

Preparing for the Story

Some steps should be taken before the earnings release.

Get the Analysts' Earnings Estimate

As stated above, before the earnings release look at zacks.com, finance.yahoo.com or another market-information website to get the analysts' consensus (or average) earnings-per-share estimate for the quarter.

Arrange to Telephone Securities Analysts

Analysts are always hard to reach on earnings day, but your chances of interviewing them will be enhanced if you can call them the day before and say you'd like to touch base after the report is released, and ask what would be a good time to call. Looking at those analysts' reports about the company—or others' reports—since the last earnings release will also help you prepare.

Look at the Prior Quarter's Earnings Story

See what numbers and issues were emphasized; they may still be relevant.

Reporting the Story

Check the Closing (4 p.m. New York Time) Price of the Stock

The price is reported (all day long, with a 20-minute lag) on those same free market-information sites. Note the gain or loss, in dollars and cents as well as in percent, from the closing price on the *previous trading day* (it could be Friday, or the day before a holiday). Do *not* use the change from today's *opening* price; it's not the same as the previous day's close, and is usually insignificant for your story.

The Press Release and Financial Statement

As we've said, read the press release carefully—and skeptically. See what the company's officers think is important; that's what they hope you'll emphasize in your story. Look for the press release's numbers in the financial statement that accompanies; company-created (i.e., non-GAAP) numbers like "adjusted earnings" or "EBITDA" probably won't be there, and thus are less important (though not necessarily to be totally disregarded, especially if the analysts attach significance to them). Find the most important numbers—**revenues (or sales)** and **net income (or earnings or profit)** and the comparative year-earlier figures; they're not always up top in the press release. Calculate the percent change from last year's quarter to this (the difference in dollars divided by the earlier figure). For net income change, use the total numbers, not per-share (EPS), because the number of shares may change from time to time, distorting the year-to-year EPS comparison (although analysts cling to it). Concentrate at first on the **statement of operations** (profit and loss) rather than the **balance sheet** (end-of-quarter statement of assets, liabilities and shareholders' equity). However, if the company is in difficulty, look on the balance sheet for changes in debt (did it increase?) and cash/securities on hand (did they drop?). Significant changes (from the prior quarter as well as from the year-ago quarter) may merit a mention in your story.

The Conference Call

Listen to the company's conference call with analysts, investors and reporters. Instructions to hear the call will be on the company's website, and probably at the bottom of the press release, too. You already know the reported numbers, so what you're looking for now is clarifications and explanations that help you tell why they're up or down, good or bad. Listen also for company comments or predictions about the quarters ahead, or for the full fiscal year. The outlook is always of interest. The conference call is public, so listen for usable quotes from the corporate officers, and perhaps even from analysts if they'll help you make a point in your story. (Caveat: know your state law on eavesdropping; in most states it's illegal to record a phone conversation unless you have an OK from all parties.)

Clarifications Needed?

If something important isn't clear to you, don't assume you're ignorant. Assume they don't know how to explain clearly, or they're spinning. So phone the company to clarify any confusion in the release or the conference call. Start with the PR department, but if you don't get the answers you need, call investor relations or the chief financial officer. Just say you don't understand a certain figure or statement or whatever, and ask them to explain it, or translate it into layman's language. An explanatory quote is especially needed when the news is bad. While you're at it, ask about jobs, always of interest. Are they hiring, or "downsizing"?

Securities Analysts

Call some analysts to get comments about the quarterly report and the company's outlook. (Collectively, analysts may be referred to as "Wall Street.") Because analysts are hard to reach on the day earnings are reported, you'll probably have to call several, and repeatedly, in order to gather a couple of good quotes. (As suggested above, it will usually be helpful to arrange these interviews the day before the earnings announcement.) As an alternative, you may quote from an analyst's post-earnings written report (a **note** or **call report**) to investors; ask the analyst's assistant or the company's PR department to e-mail it to you. In Wall Street parlance, analysts generally are considered to be on the **sell side** of the securities business, because most of them work for companies that make their money (or at least some of it) by selling stocks and bonds. On the other hand, the folks on the **buy side** are portfolio or asset managers who invest the money of big, so-called **institutional investors** like pension funds and mutual funds. These managers, too, can be good sources for your earnings story, but assume that they'll want to justify their investment in the stock, even when the quarter is disappointing.

Structuring the Story

There's no single way to write a good earnings story, but this structure won't be wrong.

The Lead (Spell It "Lede" to Avoid Confusion)

In your lede (ideally in a single sentence), state the company's name (in full, with the Inc. or Corp., on first mention) and its business, whether the profit rose or fell from the year-earlier period, with the percentage change (unless it's tiny or greater than 200 percent; then use an adjective or adverb to characterize the change), the main reason why, and whether the result was better or worse than the estimate by securities analysts. The estimate here was 3 cents a share, according to Yahoo Finance (finance.yahoo.com). Yes, that comprehensive lede is a tall order, a writing challenge, but you'll have a superb start for your story. If the stock price rose or fell 2 percent or more (compared with the previous day's closing price), say so, perhaps as a short second sentence (e.g., "The stock drooped."). If the stock move is BIG, 4 to 5 percent or more, that's the lede. A market move may be caused as much by the company's forecast of future performance as by its earnings; if so, that's in the lede, too. In this case the stock advanced to close at $31.38, up from $30.08 the day before, a gain of $1.30 or 4.3 percent.

So, a good lede for GrubHub's first quarter 2014 report would be:

> Shares of GrubHub Inc., Chicago-based provider of restaurant takeouts, leapt 4.3 percent on sharply higher earnings from surging revenues, well exceeding Wall Street expectations.

In the second and third paragraphs ("grafs"), state the end date of the quarter and the numbers, *placing the most recent numbers first*, something like this:

> Profit in the first quarter ended [not end*ing*] March 31 soared more than six times to $4.4 million, or 6 cents per diluted share, from $659,000, or 1 cent per diluted share, in the year-earlier quarter. Analysts predicted only 3 cents.
>
> Revenues jumped 49 percent to $58.6 million from $39.4 million.

At this point we need to decide whether to refer also to what the company called "non-GAAP Adjusted EBITDA," a contrived number, which rose to $16.4 million from $5.6 million in the first quarter of 2013. Since this increase, though nearly triple, doesn't contradict or undermine the big increase in actual GAAP earnings, we can omit these figures—unless analysts insist on favoring them. But that didn't happen in the company's conference call with analysts (a replay is available on the company's website).

A Helpful Quote or Two

This is an apt place to insert a good quote into your story, ideally from an analyst, but possibly from the company if it isn't mere puffery and it really helps your audience understand what happened in the quarter. In its release GrubHub had this quote and this forecast, which are informative (and we're not in a position to phone analysts for this drill anyway), so let's use them:

> "We are off to a strong start as a public company with record active diners, orders and revenues in the first quarter, continuing the robust growth momentum we had throughout 2013," stated Matt Maloney, GrubHub CEO, in a press release. "We remain focused on making takeout better by continuing product innovation, driving more orders to independent restaurants and creating more transparency and control for diners."

The Outlook

Continuing, from the press release and the conference call:

> The company predicted [in what's called **guidance**] that revenue in the second quarter end*ing* [OK when we're talking about the future] June 30 will be "in the range of $53 million to $55 million," slightly lower than in the first quarter. In the company's conference call with analysts, executives explained that GrubHub's volume always tends to dwindle somewhat in warmer weather because people are more likely to eat out than in.

Explain or Elaborate

It's appropriate here to pick up some of the "Key Pro Forma Operating Metrics" in the press release:

> GrubHub reported that its "active diners" rose in the first quarter to 3.9 million from 2.6 million a year earlier, that "daily average grubs" jumped to 181.2 million from 129.1 million, and that "gross food sales" leapt to $433 million from $300 million.

Although the conference call wasn't especially helpful to our earnings story, the CEO did comment that GrubHub will continue to emphasize television in its advertising, and that's worth a mention:

> In the conference call, CEO Maloney, responding to an analyst's question about advertising, affirmed that the company will continue to rely heavily on "national TV," inasmuch as the company operates in more than 700 markets.

The Stock

> In New York Stock Exchange trading, GrubHub's shares closed at $31.38, up $1.30.

No need to state the prior day's closing price, nor the percent gain, which we put in the lede; however, if the percent change isn't big enough to warrant using it in the lede, state it here (unless it's tiny, less than 1 percent). *Don't repeat any numbers in a business story.*

Tips

If the company reports **earnings attributable to common shareholders** or similar language (which usually indicates it paid a dividend, subtracted from profit, to holders of *preferred* stock), use that term and that number rather than net income.

If you're comparing a quarterly loss with a prior-year loss, useful verbs are "narrowed" or "widened" rather than increased or decreased. If the company moves from a profit to a loss, or vice versa, a good verb is "swung." No percentage in such cases. **N.B.**: *a decrease in profit is NOT A LOSS, it's a drop or decline in profit (or earnings).*

If you're writing about any quarter after the first, also state the earnings (total and EPS) and revenues of the longer period (two or three quarters, or full fiscal year), compared with the same period in the prior year. Those figures, too, are in the quarterly operating statement. It's helpful to repeat the date the period ended, especially if the company's fiscal year differs from the calendar year. Don't put the recent quarterly earnings (or revenues) in the same graf as the longer-period earnings (or revenues). It's confusing. Treat the periods separately, the longer period lower in the story, because the earnings news and thus the lede is always the most recent quarter, even when it's the fourth quarter.

Let's note here that a company (except a bank), as indicated above, may designate its own fiscal year, differing from the calendar year. Many do.

Retailers, for instance, end their fiscal year on or around January 31, to allow time for a post-holiday inventory. In such a case don't confuse the reader by referring to the "fiscal 2015 second quarter," which is meaningless, because a company may call an overlapping year "fiscal 2015" or "fiscal 2016" as it wishes; just write "in its second quarter ended September 30" without the calendar year, which will be obvious.

If you've followed all the above (perhaps with the help of some repeat reading), you're well prepared to write earnings stories for real, which in turn will mean you're well on the way to becoming a business reporter!

Questions for Discussion

1 Although GAAP net income is a must in every earnings story, when might you refer first to "adjusted earnings" or another non-GAAP earnings number?
2 If you have a dynamite quote from an analyst or a company officer, how high might you place it in your story?
3 Where will you place the revenues and earnings figures from any longer period covered by the earnings report?
4 If a company earns only $3 a share in this period compared with $4 a share in the year-ago period, would you report this as a profit *loss*?
5 What additional useful information can you communicate to your readers by creating a graph to accompany your story?

6 Financial Services Reporting

The earnings reports of three important industries—banking, insurance and REITs (real estate investment trusts)—differ from the standard described in Chapter 5. So our stories, while still striving to discern the same truths about the company, must differ as well.

Banks

As stated earlier, the word "bank" is commonly misused these days by both analysts and journalists, picking up Wall Street jargon that terms an investment bank a "bank." It's not.

A bank, properly referred to as a *commercial* bank, is an institution chartered by the federal government (specifically, by the Office of the Comptroller of the Currency, part of the Department of the Treasury) or a state (usually, the commissioner of banking or financial institutions) that takes deposits and makes loans. Simple. This description also applies to thrift institutions such as savings and loans, whether federal or state chartered, whose lending powers are somewhat circumscribed and focused on financing home purchases through mortgage loans.

In contrast, an *investment* bank like Morgan Stanley or JP Morgan is a different animal: it raises capital for client companies, perhaps by finding large, private investors (that might include the investment bank itself) or carrying out a public offering of the client company's securities, either stocks or bonds, to investors large and small. Most investment banks also offer securities brokerage services to the public, and they trade securities, in large amounts, for their own account, an operation that can be very lucrative.

The two "banks" have become confused (unnecessarily, with the complicity of the press) because, especially since the run-up to the Great Recession of 2007–2009, a number of large, prominent investment banks have acquired commercial banks, or have merged with a big commercial bank. Witness JP Morgan Chase & Co., or Citigroup, or Bank of America Corp., which owns the investment firm Merrill Lynch. This makes the parent corporation, or the merged corporation (the issuer of the company's securities), a **bank holding company**. Still not a bank.

In fact, the banking regulatory scheme, established by law, makes an important distinction: a federally chartered bank is supervised and regulated, and thus periodically examined, by the Office of the Comptroller of the Currency (in the Treasury Department), while a bank holding company is supervised and regulated by the Federal Reserve. The Fed, in fact, supervises and regulates any company that owns a commercial bank or a thrift institution; it, too, is a bank holding company. All commercial banks (meaning all banks) must be members of the Federal Deposit Insurance system, which means they pay premiums every year for FDIC insurance that covers their depositors' accounts up to $250,000 should the bank fail. It also means that the FDIC supervises and regulates every commercial bank, federal and state. This complex, overlapping system of regulation has been widely criticized, but it persists.

So, what does this mean for a reporter covering an earnings story? For the big banking holding companies, not much difference, but look for **chargeoffs** of defaulted or very shaky loans and the **provision for credit losses** (the "provision," a subtraction from earnings, goes into the loan loss reserve, a required buffer against future loan defaults); both are indicators of the quality of lending operations, a major source of profit for any banking institution.

Smaller Banking Companies

However, for a bank alone, or for a smaller, regional bank holding company that owns several local, community banks and carries on no investment banking or securities trading, there are these differences in their earnings reports and thus in the earnings story.

Revenues Don't Matter

They may be subordinated in your story, or even ignored. Focus on earnings.

Earnings Consist of Two Streams

1. **Net interest income**. That's the difference between the bank's cost of interest paid on deposits, and its return on loans, less the bank's provision (allowance) for loan losses. It's expressed in dollars. Another look at the profitability of lending is the **net interest *margin***, expressed in percentage points, again, the difference between interest cost and

interest earnings. A net interest margin of 4 to 5 percentage points is very good. Both net interest income and net interest margin are newsworthy; net interest *income* is essential to your story. Smaller banks tend to earn proportionally less net interest income than big banks. The big banks' earnings come primarily from lending, but that's rarely true for the little guys.

2 **Non-interest income**, or fee income, or simply "other" income. Fees charged for ATM transactions, overdrafts, wire transfers, safe deposit boxes, credit cards, asset management and so on.

Other Essentials

As with a bank holding company, look for loan chargeoffs and the provision for loan losses, and for changes in them, either up or down. Also note the total of deposits at the end of the quarter, and any change up or down; that's on the **statement of condition,** an end-of-period snapshot of assets and liabilities akin to a non-bank company's balance sheet. When people ask, "How big is that bank?" the answer is its total assets.

Although we're addressing the quarterly reports of publicly held companies here, many small, community banks are not public but owned by a relatively small number of shareholders, or perhaps by a small bank holding company that isn't public either. Nevertheless, note that financial reports of all bank holding companies, commercial banks and thrift institutions, public or private, are available from the Federal Financial Institutions Examination Council, at ffiec.gov. Or, for commercial banks, go directly to www2.fdic.gov. So, to write a story about a privately owned community bank, for instance, you don't need to depend on the bank to disclose to you its total assets or loan losses or profit or any other numbers, for they're all public.

Insurance Companies

Perhaps surprisingly, the insurance industry, including the biggest, nationwide operators, is regulated by the states, not the federal government. Each state has an insurance commissioner or similar officer who supervises and conducts examinations of the companies' operations to ascertain that they are in compliance with state insurance regulations, in particular capital requirements and reserves to cover future claims, and to assure financial stability and claims-paying ability of the companies. Note that we're speaking here primarily of insurance *underwriters* (such as Prudential Financial, Inc., MetLife, Inc. and CNA Financial Corporation), the companies that actually issue the policies and assume the risk of loss, as distinct from insurance *brokers.* The brokers (such as Marsh & McLennan Companies, Aon plc and Arthur J. Gallagher & Co.), much like *stock* brokers, are middlemen who shop for policies (mostly property and casualty policies) on behalf of clients, and, in respect to large commercial policies covering big business risks, sometimes negotiate policy terms. Brokers, too, are regulated by the states.

None of this is apparent in a company's statement of operations or even its balance sheet, unless there's a regulatory restriction or other problem, but an insurance financial report does employ some terms peculiar to the industry that should be understood and may be worth including in an earnings story. In particular, quarterly or annual reports may refer to these ratios: (1) loss ratio, (2) expense ratio, (3) dividend ratio and (4) combined ratio. They are measurements of these four kinds of costs against "net earned premiums," the premium income actually earned during the period, as opposed to "net *written* premiums," the total amount of premiums that will be received from insurance policies sold during that period.

The (1) **loss ratio** is the percentage of claims and claim adjustment expenses to net earned premiums. The (2) **expense ratio** is the percentage of underwriting and acquisition (sales) expenses to net earned premiums. The (3) **dividend ratio** is the percentage of policyholders' dividends to net earned premiums. And the (4) **combined ratio**, the most important figure, is the sum of the loss, expense and dividend ratios.

So, if the combined ratio is less than 1, the company's insurance operations are profitable. A ratio greater than 1 indicates that expenses exceeded premium revenues, i.e., an operating loss. However, the combined ratio alone doesn't necessarily mean that the company made money or lost it, for every insurance underwriter has a large investment portfolio that holds its reserves, and that portfolio may generate sufficient income to compensate for a combined ratio that's greater than 1, thus generating a net profit for the company in that period.

In most other respects a story about an insurance company's earnings follows the pattern of other companies described in the preceding chapter, so it's not necessary to repeat that exercise here.

Real Estate Investment Trusts (REITs)

Like banks, real estate investment trusts' financial statements differ significantly from the GAAP standard. They emphasize an "earnings" figure that's not according to GAAP but is generally followed by both securities analysts and the business press, often, inappropriately, to the complete neglect of GAAP net income. This peculiarity arises because real estate investment trusts, which typically own and operate numerous revenue-generating properties, enjoy an extraordinary legal advantage: they pay no federal income taxes if they pay out in dividends to their shareholders at least 90 percent of their taxable income. In fact, most pay out 100 percent. Yes, tax-free, for all intents and purposes. A gift from Congress! It was enacted in 1950 to enable small investors to obtain the tax benefits of real estate investing already available to large investors. As a result, REIT stocks are favored by investors seeking better-than-average income from their securities, as well as capital appreciation.

REITs are big business. According to the National Association of Real Estate Investment Trusts, publicly held REITs own more than $1 trillion of real estate assets in this country, comprising more than 40,000 properties in all 50 states and the District of Columbia; these REIT assets account for an estimated 15 percent of total U.S. commercial real estate assets; and REITs directly or indirectly support some 1 million U.S jobs.

The performance measurement favored by REITs is called **Funds From Operations**, or FFO. It omits major expenses and thus, like other non-GAAP "earnings" calculations, is greater than GAAP net income. Generally (but not always, for this non-GAAP term is defined differently by different REITs), here are the big items that are left out: depreciation (the required annual reduction, usually 5 percent of the purchase price, of the value of real estate shown on the balance sheet; each annual reduction is also deducted from earnings, though that subtraction isn't an actual cash loss), loan interest or amortization expense, which is usually substantial in most REIT operations (representing interest and principal reduction on mortgage borrowings to acquire properties), and profits and losses from the disposition of properties, a more or less constant feature of the operations of a large, successful REIT. The reason for frequent sales is that, because REITs must distribute their earnings to their shareholders to be tax-free, they can't accumulate profits and so, in order to acquire more properties and grow their business, they commonly resort to borrowing and to selling properties at a profit.

All of which is not to say that REITs don't report net income. They must, and they do. The reason that net income is still very important is that it determines how much the REIT will pay out in dividends, which is the principal (and tax-favored) incentive that attracts investors to REIT stocks in the first place. So your story should report both GAAP net income and FFO, with a brief explanation of how that company calculates FFO and your statement that it's a commonly used measurement of REIT performance. Then compare the reported FFO with the analysts' estimates of it, as if it were real earnings.

Like the others, these financial-services earnings stories aren't easy, particularly when a company strives to gloss over poor results and present a misleading picture. But the financial statements can't be distorted; they must conform to GAAP, so rely on them rather than concocted terms like "adjusted earnings." Still, when the analysts put great stock in the adjusted or other non-GAAP numbers, you do need to bring them into your story. If necessary, ask the company or the analysts to explain the differences and why they're emphasizing the non-GAAP.

Questions for Discussion

1 If a REIT's press release mentions only FFO, and that's all the analysts seem to care about, too, will you state the company's GAAP net income in your story? Why?
2 Which insurance-company ratio tells you whether the company's insurance operations showed a profit or a loss? Does that indicate whether the company has a net profit or a net loss?
3 How should you refer to a company that owns a commercial bank? Can you call that a bank, too?
4 How would you describe the difference between a commercial bank and an investment bank?

7 The Corporate Finance Story

Whatever a company's product or service, it's also in another business: management of its finances, and especially its cash. Every business needs cash to carry on its day-to-day operations, even if it's financially sound and can readily borrow money from a bank or sell **commercial paper**, low-interest debt obligations that come due in 30, 60 or 90 days. On the other hand, sometimes a successful company generates more cash than it needs on a daily basis, so it invests the surplus in short-term instruments like U.S. Treasury bills, which pay a little interest and can be liquidated (sold) any time the cash is needed. These short-term transactions and markets are so routine that they usually aren't newsworthy, but you'll see them reflected on a company's balance sheet, as part of **short-term** assets or liabilities, meaning they mature in a year or less.

More significant, and thus more newsworthy, are **other** or **long-term liabilities**, meaning all debts coming due after a year, because they're usually bigger and they carry interest and periodic repayment (**amortization**) obligations. Most companies have such debt, and if a company is struggling, meeting those obligations can be difficult, or, in worst cases, impossible. That means default and possibly a filing for protection from creditors in the U.S. Bankruptcy Court. (More on that in the next chapter.)

Our present focus, however, is not default but the everyday management of a healthy company's finances, especially its cash, in a way that provides adequate support for the business at minimum cost (the cost of borrowing, or perhaps interest foregone on idle, excess funds) and with some modest return from short-term investment of those excess funds.

When a company needs a lot of money, perhaps to support expected sales growth, or to buy expensive real estate or machinery, or, on a larger scale, to buy another company, assuming the amount needed exceeds what a commercial bank might lend, there are two ways to go: sell **equity** (stock) or sell **debt** (bonds or notes).

A Stock Offering

For the business seeking to raise money, there's an advantage to selling common stock rather than bonds: there's no interest obligation (although the company may choose, at its option, to pay a dividend to its shareholders). The disadvantage is that additional shares dilute the proportional ownership in the company of the existing shareholders (thus the issuance of new shares is subject to a shareholder vote), and the additional shares have the effect of reducing the company's earnings per share, an important number to securities analysts and investors. Not as common, a company also may raise money by offering shares of **preferred stock**; these shares carry a stated dividend (which keeps their price fairly constant), but they don't dilute earnings per share (nor do they have a vote at the annual shareholders' meeting).

A public offering of stock must first be registered with the Securities and Exchange Commission (or, for small, intrastate offerings, with a state securities commissioner), typically by filing a Form S-1 registration statement, or perhaps a Form S-3 or Form S-4 if the issuer is an established company. When the SEC declares the registration "effective" (which may take several weeks) the securities are immediately distributed and sold by an investment bank acting as an **underwriter**, or perhaps several underwriters in a "syndicate"; they take a healthy commission of 6 percent to 8 percent of the proceeds, in return for which they commit to buy whatever shares they can't sell to investors, so an underwritten offering poses no uncertainty for the issuer. With the distribution to the investors, public trading of the shares commences immediately on the New York Stock Exchange, the NASDAQ market, or another stock exchange or market.

A public offering of stock, or at least, an offering by an important or prominent company, may give rise to two stories: about the planned offering, usually based mostly on the registration statement; and a story about the price of the shares offered (which is not stated in the registration statement) and the results of the offering, notably the price movement in the first day of trading. Especially in an initial public offering (IPO), some "hot" stocks make a big move on the first day.

Each story about a public offering of securities needs the number of shares sold (or to be sold), the net proceeds to the company (after commissions to the underwriters), and the intended use of the funds. As always in a business story, quotes are highly desirable, in this case from underwriters, securities analysts or other market experts.

A Bond (Debt) Offering

Debt may be a loan from a bank, and that loan may have a term of as long as four or five years. But if more money, and a longer term, is required, a company has the option of selling debt securities—bonds or notes, which sometimes are backed by some sort of collateral, or security, such as a plant or equipment; or debentures, which are bonds or notes backed only by the company's promise to pay, with no collateral. The term debenture isn't much used these days, but you need to recognize it when it pops up.

Bonds or notes issued by large corporations are traded every day in the bond market, much like stocks, and their prices often, but not always, move in the opposite direction from stocks. The logic is that when stocks decline (because investors and traders are selling), the sellers may move their money into less volatile securities, bonds, which pushes their prices up. And when bond prices rise, their yield (interest) declines, because the "coupon," the company's promise to pay interest, remains constant at 5 percent or 8 percent or whatever of the original issue price (the "par value" of the bond).

Like stock offerings, a public offering of bonds is preceded by a registration statement filed with the Securities and Exchange Commission. Similarly, that document informs prospective investors of the issuer's business and its financial condition, and sets forth the risks of investing, namely that the company could encounter business problems and be unable to honor its obligations. Reflecting the quality of the bonds and the financial strength of the offeror, the bonds will be rated, starting with AAA at the top and descending to B-minus, by independent rating agencies Moody's Investors Service, Standard & Poor's, and Fitch. Just like a stock offering, a bond offering is **underwritten** by one or more investment banks that take responsibility for determining the interest rate needed to successfully market the bonds, to peddle them to investors, and to purchase any bonds left unsold. So the news stories are the same three: the offering is planned, the bonds are priced, and the bonds are sold.

If a bond issue represents a net increase in the company's total debt, it's worthwhile to ask a ratings agency or an analyst who covers the company (try a fixed-income analyst, for they specialize in analyzing debt, though it wouldn't be wrong to ask an equity analyst) to comment on whether this additional debt is a significant burden on the company's future earnings, and whether the company's stated purpose for the additional borrowing (it may simply be "for general corporate purposes") is appropriate or reasonable.

Bear in mind that states and municipalities (counties, cities, school districts, waste-water treatment districts, etc.) also issue bonds, especially to finance their capital expenditures such as new buildings or plants. These can be big and important stories, too, and since not all city-hall or education reporters have a good understanding of debt financings, it may be that these stories are assigned to business reporters. Be prepared.

So now you're wondering, why isn't there a simple writing formula for these corporate or municipal finance stories, akin to the outline laid out earlier for earnings stories? It's because the variety of story-angle possibilities is even greater, particularly if the financing reflects a major move by a major company. How do you figure that cut? The best way is to talk to securities analysts and other experts before you write. Get their take on why the story is important (and some helpful quotes), then structure and write the story accordingly. It's not your task to analyze and interpret such events. It's theirs. Just ask good questions. Follow the money.

Questions for Discussion

1 How does a reporter determine whether a stock or debt issue deserves a story, and how much of a story?
2 How would you prioritize the essential points to cover in a corporate-finance story?
3 Who's your most important source in a story about the actual sale of new securities?

8 The Bankruptcy Story

Whoa! Don't go away. Yes, this sounds arcane and obscure, but the U.S. Bankruptcy Courts, attached to each of the U.S. District Courts (the federal trial courts) around the country are a gold mine of business stories, and they're not all gloomy.

One reason is that when a company (or an individual) files a **petition for protection from creditors** in U.S. Bankruptcy Court (this federal jurisdiction is exclusive, mandated in the U.S. Constitution; there are no state bankruptcy courts), it doesn't mean the company or person is actually bankrupt. In law **bankrupt** means an entity is unable to pay its bills as they come due, or that its debts (liabilities) exceed its assets (i.e., its net worth or shareholders' equity is negative). But whether or not a company or person is legally bankrupt, filing a petition in Bankruptcy Court immediately blocks creditors from collecting or even seeking to collect money owed them. This provides welcome temporary relief for a company or person in dire financial straits, and buys time to straighten out its business and financial affairs and live to fight another day. In other words, bankruptcy in our system is intended to facilitate recovery, typically by reducing debt and perhaps by invalidating the common stock (very painful!), all of which we'll discuss in a moment.

At the same time we must recognize that in some cases a company's or a person's financial situation may be hopeless, in which case the Bankruptcy Court is able to facilitate what's called **liquidation**, but that's not as good a story, so we'll concentrate here on the rehabilitation process of a company. Big money and lots of jobs may be at stake! Good story potential!

Chapter 11

The Bankruptcy Code (federal law) is organized by chapters, and the most newsworthy chapter is Chapter 11, called **Reorganization**. It's commonly employed by the largest corporations, and in fact by any corporation that has some underlying substance, such as a good product line. General Motors and Chrysler, for instance, filed under Chapter 11. So did the parent of United Airlines, and many other companies that are still around.

The Petition-Filing Story

A company's resort to the Bankruptcy Court, though it may have been rumored or foretold, is officially launched when the company files with the clerk of the court a petition for protection from creditors. The case is commenced. A barrier against any collection effort by those creditors is immediately erected. Such a filing requires the debtor company (now officially referred to as the **debtor in possession**, because it's still running its own affairs) to lay out a detailed statement of its assets and liabilities. Like all court records, this document is public. The total of the liabilities (the debts) is a critical figure in that initial story.

As you'd expect, a publicly held corporation is obliged to notify its shareholders of its Bankruptcy Court filing. That's done by filing with the Securities and Exchange Commission a Form 8-K, which is required to inform the Commission, investors and the public of any event likely to have an important impact on the company's operations and the value of its stock. More on SEC filings later.

Stories on Bankruptcy Court Proceedings

The proceedings that follow a Bankruptcy Court filing for protection from creditors bear little resemblance to a conventional lawsuit and trial. Bankruptcy courtrooms are small, and the proceedings are highly informal, usually consisting of a lawyer, or maybe several, standing before the bankruptcy judge and discussing whatever questions or issues they want to resolve at that time. Another participant in the process, especially in a large and complex bankruptcy case, may be a **bankruptcy trustee** appointed by the judge to oversee and manage the entire proceeding. (The trustee may be the court's own full-time trustee, or an outside lawyer expert in bankruptcy.)

Bankruptcy courts, like all courts, are open to the public and the press, though usually attended only by representatives of the parties involved, including the debtor in possession and its creditors. There's no jury, no dramatic declamations by lawyers, no headline-grabbing histrionics, no dramatic unveiling of incriminating evidence.

Sometimes the complexities of the Bankruptcy Code and the negotiations require explanation—which you can provide with the help of the lawyers. The press generally pays attention only to the proceedings involving the largest companies, but there are lots of other stories—financial, legal and often very human—in Bankruptcy Court.

The Bankruptcy Story

Preparing for the Story

Try to determine in advance when you're planning to cover a hearing. Contact the lawyers for the company and creditors to ask what they'll be arguing for. One certainty: the company will seek permission to pay its usual salaries, rent and other operating expenses, and the judge will approve, so that's not a big story in itself. However, another routine company request is more newsworthy: **debtor-in-possession financing**, which is a loan or a line of credit arranged by the company with a bank or prospective investor to continue operating during the bankruptcy process. This debt will take priority over pre-bankruptcy debts; i.e., it must be paid first. The identity of that lender should be included, along with the amount of the new borrowings, in your story. This borrowing, and all other significant financial transactions by the debtor in possession, requires advance approval by the bankruptcy judge.

Prepare to cover any bankruptcy hearing. Familiarize yourself with the case and the company. Tell the lawyers in advance that you'll cover the hearing, and ask them what issues will be discussed. In the courtrooms, which are small, there's usually no sound amplification or video recording, so sit in the front row, listen closely and take good notes. No recording permitted. You'll probably see the lawyers you've contacted approach the bench and identify themselves. If you don't understand what's happening, particularly if the judge rules on some disputed issue, buttonhole the lawyers during a break and get an explanation. Usually they're happy to have any coverage and to make their points to the press.

Others attending a bankruptcy hearing may be high-ranking officers of the companies involved—sometimes even the chief executive officer or the chief financial officer. Know their names in advance, bring their photos with you if possible, and don't hesitate to approach them during a break. A rare opportunity to question the top dogs! They, too, will probably be happy to emphasize and explain what they're asking the judge to do.

The object of these hearings is to develop a **plan of reorganization**—by reducing debt and bringing in new capital—that all parties and the judge can agree on. Chapter 11 empowers the judge to void, or cancel, any debts or other legal obligations the company has, including union contracts. These are truly extraordinary actions. This can be hard on employees, contractors, suppliers, anyone who has provided goods or services to the company and hasn't been paid. And shareholders are at risk. To reduce the company's obligations, the court typically will adopt a **cramdown** of investors' and lenders' claims, and holders of common stock are the first to be axed. Their interest in the company may be reduced or entirely canceled, with creditors (bondholders and lenders) sometimes taking control of the company by exchanging their IOUs for new common stock.

The bankruptcy process may take only a few days, particularly if the troubled company, even before filing its petition, has found new investors or perhaps agreed to be acquired by a larger company. On the other hand, the process may take months, sometimes even years, especially if the debtor company seeks to abrogate its union contracts, which inevitably stirs up a hornet's nest. The unions, of course, will push back hard, and their lawyers will participate in the bankruptcy hearings. Other lawyers participating will represent the shareholders, secured creditors (lenders whose debts are backed by collateral of some sort) and unsecured creditors (without collateral, which includes trade creditors such as office supply retailers, trash removal services, and other small businesses, usually forced to settle for pennies on the dollar).

Reporting the Story

In their hearings the lawyers and the judge will carry on informal conversations across the bench, debating motions offered by one party or another, offering point and counterpoint, calling officials and outside experts to testify on this or that, always working toward resolving differences without yielding too much. Eventually, sooner or later, they'll arrive at a consensus that will end the case.

Another possible news source about a bankruptcy case (or perhaps a near-death experience that gets resolved without the bankruptcy filing): experienced business managers, commercial lawyers, accountants and other professionals who are hired by a troubled company (more likely a smaller, privately held company) to help resurrect it, perhaps even to run the company for a time. These recovery specialists have their own professional organization, the Turnaround Management Association, with chapters in principal cities.

Is it appropriate to write stories along the way, apart from court hearings, about the people affected—or likely to be affected—by a company's bankruptcy filing? Of course it is. You'll get good story ideas from the hearings, names of individuals and small companies, for instance, whose claims are being held up, or maybe canceled entirely.

Structuring the Story

Once a reorganization plan has been agreed to by all parties concerned, including the judge, and then formally approved by the judge in final, written form, the company is **discharged** from bankruptcy, freeing it to return to the fray in full control of its own operations and finances. That's the lede. A story about the reorganization plan and the discharge, of course, needs numbers, about reductions of debt or other financial commitments, about any changes in union contracts or other legal obligations, and about any changes in ownership or management of the company. They may be substantial! Talk to the lawyers to make sure you're getting all important aspects of the reorganization plan, especially whatever damage is done to the various categories of creditors and the shareholders.

Chapter 13

This is the **wage-earner's bankruptcy**, for individuals only, and typically for persons who have a job and reasonable hope of getting back on their feet. This probably will need the cooperation of creditors. They may consent to a stretch-out of debt repayment, or even a reduction of debt. As in corporate bankruptcy, a case is commenced by the filing of a petition for protection from creditors. Unless the person is a celebrity, an individual case is not likely to be a story. The result of each case is typically a court-mandated reduction in debts, all except the home mortgage loan, which must still be honored and paid. The debtor may lose his car, but is able to keep the house. The downside is that the debtor's credit rating is all but ruined, usually for seven years.

U.S. Bankruptcy Court clerks, who are the professional administrators of these courts, keep excellent records and compile statistics about the number of cases filed (separated by companies and individuals). These numbers, which are public, often make a worthwhile news story, particularly the Chapter 13 numbers. You can obtain national figures or local court figures. Get some quotes from bankruptcy lawyers or personal financial counselors, and you have a story, without prying into anyone's embarrassing personal affairs. By the way, the court clerks probably won't comment on their data, but they're usually helpful in making their records available and guiding a reporter through them, especially if you go to their office and introduce yourself in person.

Chapter 7

Debtors, either companies or individuals, who have no hope of regaining their footing may opt for Chapter 7 **liquidation**, or may be forced into it by the court, no matter what chapter has been invoked in the petition. That unhappy result means the debtor must liquidate, or sell, all his assets, and use the proceeds to satisfy his creditors to the extent that he can, as determined by the court. The debtor is relieved of any further obligations to his creditors, but will have a hard time getting a credit card or a loan.

Chapter 9

Now here's a sleeper. Chapter 9 covers bankruptcies by municipalities—cities, towns, counties, school districts, park districts, any public taxing body or special-purpose corporation established by a municipality, such as an incinerator operator. Detroit is not the only municipality forced to file Chapter 9, and, with the universal overpromising of pension benefits by state and local governments over many years, their obligations are simply insuperable. In September 2014 Moody's Investors Service estimated that just the 25 biggest municipal defined-benefit pension funds had unfunded pension liabilities approaching $2 trillion. Although it's a touchy subject to be avoided politically, it appears likely that there will be many more Chapter 9s as taxpayers are pitted against public employees and municipal-bond holders in no-win contests. Note that a Chapter 9 case may be filed only if your state law authorizes such filings; if there's no such law and there are municipalities in your state in deep financial trouble, watch for such a bill to be introduced and perhaps enacted by your legislature. That's a story in itself, easily overlooked by a statehouse reporter distracted by more prominent stories.

Tips

Though bankruptcy court may appear to be mysterious, forbidding territory for most reporters, even business reporters, it's obviously a fruitful field to cultivate. You'll flush out stories that most reporters will miss. Get acquainted with the clerk of the U.S. Bankruptcy Court that serves your locale. Ask him or her to point out big or otherwise interesting cases in progress, and to alert you to future filings that might be newsworthy. Then check in with the clerk's office from time to time. They'll probably welcome your interest, quite unusual among journalists. Then make the calls to the lawyers and other experts that will enable you to frame and interpret each story so that laymen will understand it.

Questions for Discussion

1 When is the best time to start covering a bankruptcy case?
2 What sources should be consulted before covering a Bankruptcy Court hearing?
3 Identify local-area municipalities (including special districts, such as school districts) that have the largest unfunded pension liabilities, and ask whether they're contemplating filing a Chapter 9 bankruptcy case. Even if they're not, you may have a story that dismisses the possibility.

9 The Corporate Outlook Story

To become a competent business reporter you must delve into publicly held companies on your beat, and most business beats are built around industries or clusters of such public companies. Covering a company can be a daunting task, especially in the case of a vast corporation with billions or even hundreds of billions of dollars in annual sales. How to proceed?

A good initial undertaking is to write a story on the company's prospects for the next year or so, as seen by the securities analysts who cover the company. This gives you solid, respected sources to draw on, but at the same time requires you to examine the company's finances and operations through its recent quarterly and annual reports.

Preparing for the Story

Pick a company, perhaps in your locale, that's covered by several analysts. (Some companies will list their analysts on the company's Web page.) If the company is in trouble, or has just undergone a major event such as an acquisition or divestiture, or installed a new chief executive officer, that's a good reason to pick it, and a good news peg to hang your story on.

What Do Analysts Expect?

Most analysts work for investment companies that underwrite securities offerings and endeavor to sell securities to their customers, both institutional (banks, insurance companies, mutual funds, pension funds, etc.) and individual. These analysts are on the **sell side**, in the jargon of Wall Street. (On the other hand, asset managers, who invest large sums for pension funds, university endowments and other such huge clients, are on the **buy side**.) Obviously, sell-side analysts are always on the lookout for shares of companies, large or small, that seem to hold promise for appreciation, typically based on the company's expected future earnings growth, so that the analysts (and the brokers in their firms) can recommend these stocks to their customers.

Analysts, who typically specialize in covering companies in just a single industry such as transportation or banking or manufacturing, proclaim their judgments about each company in several ways, such as quarterly earnings forecasts, setting a target price or prediction (usually one year ahead) for the stock, rating the stock as **buy**, **sell** or **hold** (or words to that effect, like **accumulate**, **neutral** or **underweight**), comparing the price/earnings ratio of the stock (both figures stated on a per-share basis) to the overall market or to competitor companies, all of these incorporated into an occasional detailed textual analysis of the company, its current business, opportunities, problems and prospects. These reports and projections carry great weight with investors and traders, so much that sometimes when a single analyst changes his or her rating of a stock (say, from hold to buy, or vice versa), the market reacts immediately with a swing in the stock's price.

Earnings Forecasts

Most analysts will estimate a company's quarterly per-share earnings for the next four to six quarters. You may obtain these forecasts from the analysts (or their assistants or their firm's public information office), or from investment-data websites such as Yahoo Finance or Zacks. They're subject to change at any time, of course.

The earnings forecast is the single most important number that an analyst generates, but, to emphasize comments about company earnings reports in Chapter 5, caution: the forecast may, properly, represent net income per share, whose calculation is governed by the accounting profession's **Generally Accepted Accounting Principles (GAAP)** and required by the Securities and Exchange Commission; but sometimes it doesn't, and the distinction may not be entirely clear. Again, it's quite common these days for a company to emphasize in its quarterly press release some other measure of "earnings," not a GAAP figure but what the company may call "adjusted earnings" or "earnings before one-time charges," or "earnings before items." Of course, the company itself defines these deviant "earnings," which typically exclude certain costs or expenses that depress earnings, such as the legal and other expenses of acquiring another company, or the losses of subsidiaries now targeted for sale (even though they're still part of the company; this incomplete figure would be called "earnings from continuing operations"). Of course, these figments of the imagination always look better than GAAP net income, which the company still must report in its quarterly operating statement if not in its press release. Find it!

Unfortunately, and surprisingly, analysts sometimes go along with the company's fudging of its earnings. Without saying so, they may announce estimates that aren't according to GAAP, but according to some distortion favorable to the company.

For instance, as mentioned earlier, one deviation is called **Earnings Before Interest, Taxes, Depreciation and Amortization**, or **EBITDA**. Obviously, every company must pay interest on its debts (almost every company has debt) and income taxes (assuming it's profitable). These are real, cash outlays. At the same time, there's no cash outlay involved in Depreciation (recording the year-by-year loss of value of assets such as buildings and equipment, the losses to be subtracted from earnings as well as from assets on the balance sheet) or in Amortization (a similar year-by-year diminution of financial obligations). However, a financially strong, well-managed company should be investing in new plant and equipment each year an amount roughly equivalent to its depreciation of such assets, so the exclusion of Depreciation in crowing about EBITDA is still deceptive.

Another distortion, even fuzzier, is "adjusted earnings" or "earnings before one-time items" or simply "earnings before items." Or, if you can believe it, "adjusted EBITDA." These figures (again, always favorable to the company) stray farther and farther from the truth. The company simply defines these "earnings" any way it pleases! Yet, if it persists and talks primarily in these misleading terms, both in earnings releases and management's conference calls with analysts after the releases, the analysts, lamentably, sometimes go along and estimate such distortions rather than GAAP net income. As stated earlier, these misleading figures may not be clearly identified as non-GAAP, notably in the compilations of earnings estimates by data services such as Yahoo Finance and Zacks.

What's a conscientious journalist to do?

Ask an analyst: What were you guys estimating? For some reason, the analysts tend to move together, i.e., they'll all estimate GAAP net earnings, or they'll all glom on to something else, the same company-defined "adjusted" earnings or other obfuscation.

However, if you can't reach an analyst immediately to ask what "earnings" they're all estimating, take a look at the analysts' consensus estimate, and compare it with the true GAAP earnings reported by the company, as well as its "adjusted" figure. Is the analysts' consensus closer to the GAAP or the "adjusted"? For instance, if the analysts' consensus is $1 a share, and the company reports GAAP net income of 70 cents but "adjusted earnings" of $1.02, it's pretty clear the analysts were estimating "adjusted," even if they didn't explicitly say so.

This check may be useful in doing your quarterly earnings story, and it's also useful in the corporate outlook story, because in writing either story you need the analysts' consensus estimate (and probably the estimates of individual analysts you quote, as well). When the company and the analysts use an earnings figure other than GAAP, you'll want both in your story.

Ratings of the Stock (Buy, Sell, Hold)

This, too, is a crucial element in your corporate outlook story. But the ratings are rarely unanimous, setting the stage for some contrary quotes from analysts, a skeptical element that's desirable in any business story. Particularly if one or two analysts are outliers from the pack, for instance, bestowing "sell" ratings when most other analysts say "buy," getting explanations or reasoning from the naysayers is absolutely essential. Why do they think the new CEO is talking nonsense when others praise his or her vision? Why do they think the new South American strategy is a loser when others deem it a slam dunk? Their thinking, as well as the thoughts of the other analysts, may be apparent in their published comments, or "notes," but a personal interview is always better: more spontaneous expression, less stilted and probably less cautious. Another aspect of analysts' ratings to probe in reporting the corporate outlook story is the reasoning behind any recent change in the rating, either up or down. As stated earlier, even a single analyst's change can trigger a stock market reaction. So what caused the analyst to change his or her mind about the stock (and, presumably, about the company)?

Incidentally, if the analysts make comments critical of the company or its management, comments you want to use in your story, call the company's press office and ask for a rejoinder. If you have to leave a message requesting a callback, spell out the specific reason for your call, stating the criticism you intend to use. Do that at least twice. That way, if the company never returns your calls (not good PR, but it happens), you can write in good conscience, "the company didn't return calls seeking comment," or words to that effect.

Target Price of the Stock

Most analysts try to predict where each stock they cover is headed over the next 12 months or so. They state a specific target price. In fact, their success (or lack of it) in such prognostication gives rise to annual rankings of the analysts covering each major industry. Like ratings changes, any change in an analyst's target price is a good reason to ask for an explanatory comment.

Analysts' Reports on the Stock

These analyst reports, sometimes dubbed "call reports" (especially right after an earnings report and conference call) or simply "notes," are usually quite detailed and sometimes voluminous. They typically set forth the company's recent numbers and the analyst's comments and predictions about the next year or so. Some reports (including all 30 companies in the Dow Jones Industrial Average) are at valueline.com, or, for a comprehensive, searchable database, through your college library: Value Line Investment Survey. Or, simply ask an analyst who covers the company, or her assistant, or the firm's public relations office, to send you the analyst's most recent report on the company. They're quotable (with full credit, of course), though often the language is stilted or laced with Wall Street jargon or abbreviations that may be better paraphrased.

SEC Filings

Perusing the company's most recent filings with the Securities and Exchange Commission is a must. Most companies will link to them through their website's "Investor Relations" or something similar. Or they're available at the sec.gov "Edgar" database. Read, but don't get bogged down in them. They're detailed and thick. A good section to focus on is "Management's Discussion and Analysis," a text that explains and discusses important aspects of the company's operations, including problems and challenges. This text may cause you to refer to the accompanying financial statements, but you've already seen them in the quarterly earnings releases, so by themselves they may not have much new information for you. However, the footnotes to the financial statements may indeed provide useful fresh information that you'll want to pursue with the company or the analysts. Following are the reports that are most likely to be helpful.

Form 10-K

This is the annual report, thickest of them all. It usually isn't filed until several months after the end of the company's fiscal year (which isn't necessarily December 31), because annual financial statements must be audited by an outside accounting firm before publication, and that takes time.

Form 10-Q

This is the quarterly report. An audit is not required (thus the financial statements will be labeled "unaudited"), so the report comes out sooner after the period's end—generally just a few weeks—than the annual report does. However, the 10-Q is rarely produced as quickly as the quarterly earnings announcement, so it's no help to you on the earnings story, but it may well contain useful, newsworthy information that both you and other reporters lacked in covering the earnings. Worth a look. N.B.: there's no 10-Q for a company's fourth quarter; those results are provided only through a company year-end press release (and the fourth quarter is the focus of your year-end story, rather than the annual results, though they're included).

Form 8-K

This is not a periodic report. It's required whenever something occurs that may affect the company, or the market's view of it. For instance, the sudden death of the chief executive officer, or a merger agreement just reached, or a tax ruling, whether adverse or favorable, by the Internal Revenue Service. Through an overabundance of caution, some 8-Ks, as you'll see, deal with trivia that has no news value. But at least glance at the company's most recent 8-K filings before you write your corporate outlook story.

Schedule 14A

This form, filed annually (generally in a preliminary form, and then a final, **Schedule DEF 14A**), contains the company's announcement of its annual shareholders' meeting and an invitation to shareholders who can't attend the meeting (most can't) to cast a proxy vote, for election of directors, to ratify the company's appointment of the outside auditor, and for whatever else is on the meeting agenda requiring a shareholder vote. For instance, individual shareholders' resolutions, often dealing with environmental protection or lab animal rights or similar issues with a public interest, may be on the agenda. Though these resolutions don't win if management recommends a vote against them (it always does), such resolutions may have some news value. However, the Schedule 14A's principal news value, in many instances, is the required disclosure of the compensation of the company's top officers. That story was probably written immediately at the time the 14A was filed, perhaps weeks or months before you're writing your corporate outlook story, but it's still worth a look as general background. (And next year watch for Schedule 14A when it's filed, probably a story there!)

Schedule 13D

Notice of acquisition of 5 percent ownership of a publicly held company. This may be a tipoff that the buyer seeks to take control of the company, either by further stock purchases or by acquisition. It doesn't take

51 percent to control a public company with millions of shares outstanding. Just an apparently tiny wedge may suffice, if not to take voting control, to pressure the management to adopt an unwanted policy, such as a merger or divestiture.

Form 144

Notice of sale of stock by an insider (officer, director or major shareholder). Such transactions may indicate how a seller feels about the outlook for his own company.

Schedule 14D1F

Notice of a tender offer for securities (an offer to buy them). This likely reflects an effort to take control of a company.

Reporting the Story

Though analysts seem to be harder and harder to reach these days, live quotes from a personal interview are clearly a strength of any corporate outlook story (as in any news story). Know your subject and your questions before phoning. If something the company or the analyst herself has said is unclear but seems important, don't hesitate to ask simply, "How should I define that term?" or "Can you put that in layman's language for me?" And remember to phone the company to respond to any adverse material you intend to use.

Talk to more than one analyst. Zero in on any significant differences in their ratings of the stock, their earnings forecasts or their target prices for the stock. Why? What do they see as weaknesses of the company, or its strengths, that are important in their assessments of its future?

Structuring the Story

Now you've done your reporting, assembling all the relevant information, much more than you can possibly fit into a single story. But your story isn't to be encyclopedic. Leave that to the analysts. Your purpose is to construct a story that has a message, a purpose, a point, like any good news story. So, before you even start to sort through your material, step back from it for a few moments. What emerges in your mind as the most important finding of your reporting? What do the analysts expect of this company in the foreseeable future? Expansion and growth?

Just muddling along? Facing a major competitive test? When you formulate your principal message, write it down, just a few words, then jot down three or four points—still from your general overview of your reporting—that will enable you to support that principal message. That's your outline. As you write, it may prove to be absolutely perfect, or it may warrant revision, but at least it's a plan that will guide you through a purposeful exhuming of details from your reporting. Selectively use the company numbers, the analysts' projections, findings from the SEC filings and your interview quotes to put muscle on the skeleton of your outline.

The Lede

Try writing more than one possible lede, all of them devoted to the same purpose: to summarize succinctly, perhaps even colorfully, the main message that you've formulated. This traditional approach, the pyramid style, may grate a bit. When you've gathered an abundance of material, and you're not on deadline, there's a natural temptation to "write," to be more creative with your lede, maybe conjure up a metaphor or a simile, or seize on a particularly good quote or example that makes your main point in an anecdotal lede. There's no wrong or right here. However, as audience attention spans shrink in the face of information overload (think of your own reading habits), the chance of engaging readers is enhanced by stating immediately what's most important, thus encouraging them to read further.

Look Ahead

State each point undergirding the lede, in order of importance, then support each one as effectively as you can, drawing from all of your reporting. As always, quotes are more than desirable, they're absolutely essential, so strive to get a quote or two as high in the story as you can.

Caution: *do not* excise material that fails to support your message, or maybe even contradicts it. Indeed, welcome it. This is important. Good journalism, even when you want to make a point, includes adverse material. Just as trial lawyers must acknowledge contrary evidence and try to minimize its significance, your adverse material can properly be presented in a paragraph that starts something like, "To be sure, not all analysts share this view…," or "It's worth noting the downside [or the risks] of this strategy…." And don't relegate such a paragraph to the bottom of your story; you want it read. It tells the reader that this is conscientious, balanced journalism, not a slanted advocacy piece.

Tips

There are real fringe benefits to writing the corporate outlook story, especially if you're new to the beat. It forces you to delve more deeply into a company's finances and operations, its SEC filings, its industry and analysts' thinking about the specific company and their general modus operandi. And you may see a spark of another story, perhaps a business trend story, the real mark of a savvy, observant reporter. This story is a lot of work, so as you plow through it, you should pick up other ideas and identify sources you can readily return to for future stories.

Questions for Discussion

1 What's a public company on your beat that you'd like to learn more about? Why? Is there a good news peg available? (Lack of one doesn't necessarily torpedo the story.) Has anybody published a good story about the company's outlook recently?
2 If your chosen company is followed by several analysts, and they're not of one mind, how many do you need to incorporate in your story to make it authoritative?
3 What kind of analyst comment or rating would necessitate a call to the company for a rejoinder?

10 The Economic Indicator Story

Economic indicators are statistical reports from the government or authoritative private organizations such as The Conference Board or the National Association of Realtors (both are business organizations, with an interest, to be sure) that measure some aspect of the economy. For instance: employment and unemployment, gross domestic product (GDP, the sum total of the nation's output of goods and services), consumer price index (CPI), new housing starts, real estate sales, industrial production, consumer confidence, and so on.

Preparing for the Story

The indicator releases are listed well in advance at biz.yahoo.com, and they arrive in a steady flow throughout the year, so you can write one of these stories almost any day. Usually the releases provide much more data than can be used in an ordinary news story, so the challenge is to select the essential data and present it clearly, along with interpretive quotes by economists or other experts.

Some Special Terms

Typically one or more of these terms must be included in your story, to help understand the numbers.

> **Estimated** Gross domestic product and other indicators published by government agencies often are **estimated (or preliminary)**, then later (most likely one month later) **revised**. Use the adjective the government does. So if you're also looking at the month-earlier report (perhaps to create a graph), and it refers to its reported number as **estimated**, remember to substitute for it the **revised** figure in the current-month report.

Seasonally adjusted Some statistics are modified to smooth out normal seasonal fluctuations. For instance, construction slows in the winter, therefore home starts or other construction indicators are commonly adjusted so that a normal seasonal upswing in the spring and summer months isn't over-interpreted as a real improvement. When the source labels its figures **seasonally adjusted**, be sure to say that in your story. If your report provides both seasonally adjusted and unadjusted figures, use the seasonally adjusted.

Annual rate This is the emphasis in some statistical reports, rather than the raw monthly or quarterly numbers. Like a seasonal adjustment, the annual rate is intended to portray a more accurate picture of economic activity. If the numbers you're using are **annual rates**, say so. For example, monthly home sales are expressed as so many units, at an annual rate.

Real This means the numbers are adjusted to eliminate any distortion that might be caused by inflation, again to portray a more accurate picture of economic activity. If your report provides both **nominal** (the actual, raw numbers) and **real** numbers, use the latter, and state it.

Index An index isn't a measure of dollars or tons or anything real; it's a mathematical construct designed to indicate change over a long period of time, based on a measurement established in a **base year** that's assigned the starting index number of 100. Sometimes the base year is represented in this fashion: 1985 = 100. Except when referring to a very prominent, common index such as the Standard & Poor's 500 Stock Index, whenever you write a story about an index, state that base year. (By the way, the also very prominent **Dow Jones Industrial Average**, or **DJIA**, is just that, an *average* of the prices of 30 major stocks, adjusted over the years for stock splits and for the substitution of new stocks for old from time to time; it must not be referred to as an index.)

Percent or percentage points? When you express a statistical change in percentage terms, think twice before you write **percent** or **percentage points**. A change in an index number or a dollar amount is stated as a percent change, e.g., 3.2 percent. But for a report given in percents, your story should state changes in **percentage points**. For example, interest rates and inflation rates are percents, so changes are in percentage points. Corollary: don't express *a change in percents* as a percent.

Compare with This means you're comparing a new figure with an earlier figure measuring the same phenomenon, housing starts, for instance. **Compare to** is used to contrast two *dissimilar* numbers or phenomena, such as U.S. GDP and China's. For most economic indicators, report the change from the previous month (the sequential, period-to-period change), using **compare with**. That's because, especially as the

U.S. economy recovered from the Great Recession, the focus was on month-to-month (or quarter-to-quarter) change However, sometimes it's informative to compare the new number with the year-earlier month as well (the year-over-year change). When in doubt, do both, leading with the month-to-month.

Core Some reports provide a stripped-down version of an indicator, removing volatile components. For instance, the **consumer price index (CPI)** release also states the **core CPI**, which omits food and energy (gasoline, heating oil, etc.), because their variations can obscure the underlying trend in the cost of living. When the report cites a **core** number, use it, and label it as such, but use the overall number, too.

Choose your economic indicator in advance. Note the time of the release; it's always early in the day, which is a help. Try to line up a couple of economists in advance: "Could I call you when the GNP figure comes out tomorrow morning?" Expert opinion is absolutely necessary to explain and interpret economic data. Until you become a free-wheeling columnist, leave this to the pros—economists (either in business, e.g., banks, or academia), business consultants, and trade or professional associations like the National Association of Manufacturers or the National Retail Merchants Association. Search profnet.com for experts (or submit to profnet.com your own specific inquiry, stating what you're writing and what kind of expert you want to interview, and your deadline), and most universities' press offices will be pleased to recommend professors with expertise on the subject you're covering. If you're looking to inject some local flavor into a national indicator story, the experts can help you do that, perhaps reflecting on the local implications of the big picture. Look up the previous number, for last month or last quarter or last year. What happened then, and why? To help answer those questions, find a story about that release by Reuters or AP or another reputable organization, Note the lede and the flow of the story. You could do worse than imitate the pros, especially when you're new to economic indicators.

Finally, find the consensus forecast, usually derived from a poll of economists, of the indicator that's about to be released. You'll want to compare the new number with that forecast. If there's a significant difference, it may well move the stock market.

Reporting the Story

Read the press release carefully. Note whether the number is nominal (current dollars) or real (inflation-adjusted), whether it's an estimate or final, whether it's for that month or that quarter, or expressed as an annual rate.

When you understand what the release says, call the economists for interpretation and comments. This isn't easy at first. But it's necessary, and it usually proves to be a satisfying learning experience, tapping into the wisdom of expertise. Academic economists (actual teachers, not just researchers) may be more patient than a busy corporate economist who's trying to write a report for his bosses. In any event, you can get started by asking simply, "What did you think of the unemployment announcement?" Then you'll want to follow up on whatever your economist says, and that's where your knowledge of the release will come in handy. Are there any contrary signs or sub-themes in the report? Finally, ask for a forecast: what's next month or next quarter going to bring? Why? Then call another economist and repeat the drill; it's sometimes surprising how experts' interpretation of the same data can differ.

Structuring the Story

Choose and describe the most telling numbers in your lede. This probably will be obvious, largely because that's the focus of the press release that accompanies the numbers. But look also for any sub-themes in the release or in the data, for instance, hints of contrary economic winds that are beginning to blow, and don't neglect them in your story.

Your lede should incorporate the expert interpretation along with the numbers or at least what the numbers convey. For example:

> The growth of the nation's output of goods and services—the gross domestic product—slowed sharply to a seasonally adjusted annual rate of 1.5 percent in the third quarter, according to the advance estimate by the Department of Commerce. GDP grew 3.9 percent in the previous quarter. The slowdown was expected, and the stock market dipped only slightly.

Tips

As with the corporate outlook story, watch the economic indicators for trend story ideas. For instance, you might develop a consumer angle by interviewing local residents about their jobs or their shopping habits or their personal financial confidence. (Of course, if you're nimble, you might even incorporate some consumer interviews into your indicator story itself.) All business stories have such a human side, always worth cultivating.

Questions for Discussion

1 Suppose you're writing the gross domestic product story, reporting a quarterly gain in the nation's total output of goods and services. What question(s) will you ask the experts, and what question(s) can you formulate to incorporate some man-on-the-street quotes into your story?
2 How do you decide whether to compare a new economic statistic with the prior period or with the year-earlier period? Or, if both comparisons are informative, which to feature in your lede?
3 What's the difference between **real** and **estimated**? Why are these adjectives important?

11 The Small Business Story

To be deemed solid business journalism, the small business story should not degenerate into a lifestyle paean or a fawning celebration of success, especially without vital numbers. Small business is serious business, and a successful one is a legitimate subject of reader interest. In the highly competitive marketplace that is the American economy, success doesn't just happen; it's far from automatic. Somebody drives it.

Preparing for the Story

To make your story, your chosen subject must be helpful, by providing photo access and numbers and other vital information about the business. Many small-business owners consider such information absolutely private. Accordingly, tell the owner up front that you'll need numbers, particularly annual revenues, so you don't waste your time gathering other information only to find that you won't get the essentials. If your subject demurs, then, no matter how fascinating the business concept or how personable the owner, move on to someone who wants to cooperate.

How do you identify an appropriate subject? Mostly by keeping your eyes open. Look for shops, restaurants, service providers like dog washes or insurance brokers (is it too soon to suggest drone delivery services?), local Internet operations or other visible businesses that appear successful. A little quirkiness can be attractive, too. Think photo or video possibilities. But rule out the new ventures, businesses less than a year old. They don't yet have enough track record to be deemed successful. Most small businesses fail, so let the marketplace assist you in finding the newsworthy exceptions. On occasion a small business that wants publicity will send out a press release or launch a promotion, and if it's already a solid business, not a startup, that initiative may identify an owner who will respond to a reporter's probing questions.

Caution: this story cannot be done on the phone. It's vital to visit the company, to obtain face-to-face interviews, scene descriptions, and photos or video.

Numbers

As with all business stories, numbers are essential. Two are especially telling: annual revenues and the current number of employees, and the trends in both. Are they flat, increasing, decreasing? By what percent? Even a successful business will encounter occasional speed bumps, so cutting staff or even losing sales isn't necessarily a disqualification, for your purposes. In fact, how the business deals with adversity and surprise will lend authenticity to your story.

Although profit is a vital element of a big-business story, it's not essential here. For one thing, it's a highly confidential figure and you're not likely to get it, so no need to make an issue of it. Also, the profit of a small business, even a very good one, can seem disarmingly small, because owners can maximize expenses (and thus minimize profit, and taxes) by paying themselves generous salaries and by deducting business-related expenses like entertainment and use of a personal auto.

To explore and imagine photo possibilities, arrange with the owner's assistant or the marketing/PR person to arrive 15 to 30 minutes before your appointment to look around the premises for locations and natural light. A factory or warehouse offers myriad potential. But even a corridor or blank wall may work, too—if the lighting is adequate.

Reporting the Story

Besides getting the essential numbers, ask the owner what makes the business successful. Creative people? Good products? Precise engineering? Effective marketing? Quick turnaround of customers' orders? If the answer is very broad, like "we give good service," press for details and examples. If the shop worked through a holiday and the owner personally drove the new part overnight to a distant customer, that's a winner for you as well as for him.

Lots of successful small-business owners (like successful executives of big companies) are engaging personalities, warm and enthusiastic, really fascinating people, fun to meet and interview. But don't let yourself be beguiled by them. If they express generalities, for instance, that the business "runs itself," or that it fulfills his or her need "to be creative," press for explanations, details, examples. And if afterwards you realize you need more such substantive details to support a point in your story, don't hesitate to call back.

A little history of the business, particularly if it's decades-long and perhaps in the third or fourth generation of a family, will be helpful to your story. But your story is not a chronology, and year-by-year details, or even decade-by-decade, are boring reading, so this background will need to be relatively brief and incorporated more artfully.

Photos/Video

Your photos and/or video should add to the story in a complementary way. For instance, if the business is a machine shop or other manufacturer, you'll surely want scenes of the shop, with workers on the job. (If it's a close-up, get their names.) If it's an Internet or office-only business, like an accounting or marketing firm, for instance, you'll have to be imaginative. Look for unusual angles or lighting. More on photography in a moment.

Although you should strive to illustrate your story with more than the owner's photo, by all means get it while you're there. However, posing the owner seated at her desk or her computer or holding a phone is terribly trite. Perhaps picture her in conversation with an associate, or gazing out the window, or explaining an important product.

Quotes

An interview of the owner may well provide the core information for your story, and perhaps a good visual if you're doing the story primarily or partially in video. If it's primarily a text story with a video interview as a sidebar, the video shouldn't merely repeat or duplicate the text. Cut the video to supplement the story, to enlarge or add to it.

It's also important to broaden the story beyond the owner interview; one-source stories, on any subject, rarely constitute good journalism. Other quotes may be obtained at the company from other officers, who may be family members, or perhaps long-time employees in the office, shop or warehouse.

Most helpful to your story are interviews with customers or clients. If you're writing about a shop or a community bank or other business open to the public, it's easy to interview customers as they come and go, perhaps on the street if the owner objects to your distracting customers as they shop. But the customers of other businesses, like a manufacturer or professional services provider (an advertising firm, for instance), won't be so readily available, so ask the owner to provide a few names of people you might interview for your story. The owner will probably want to check with the customers before providing their names, and that's OK. Ask the customers why they do business with this company, and for examples of the company's consideration for its customers. Of course, this approach isn't likely to produce a cross-section of the firm's customers. The owner will surely identify only satisfied customers, perhaps long-time users of the company's goods or services, but interviewing them is far better than having no customers at all, or writing a one-source story. They'll help broaden and balance your story, and perhaps provide a good quote you can use high in the story, as suggested below.

Missteps

Another way of broadening and balancing is to ask the owner, after letting him or her boast about the firm's strengths, accomplishments and track record, about mistakes or missteps along the way. Every business has them. Did a new product bomb? Did an important hire flub the job? Did an advertisement backfire? Get enough details so you can include the gaffe in your story.

Other Sources

In addition to other company voices and those of customers, consider whether an expert in that business or industry might have something to contribute to your story, such as an observation about the state of competition in the industry, or changes taking place in it. Even if they know that industry, securities analysts won't comment for a story about a privately owned company, but there may be a trade or professional association with a good overview of the industry, and business-school teachers and business consultants who specialize in that industry are other possible sources.

Structuring the Story

By definition, a small-business story may not be one your audience considers important. So how do you attract their attention—and hold it? An arresting, engaging lede is essential. Your lede could be like that of a hard-news story, a tight, crisp summary of your message, which probably tells why this company is successful in a competitive marketplace. But there's room for creativity here.

The lede could be anecdotal, a quick telling of an incident or event that's a microcosm of your message. Or you could start with an expressive quote, from the owner or a customer. Again, it should faithfully convey the message of the story, and that's what makes this business a good one. A quote or anecdote that's cute but off-message will not work as a lede.

What Makes This Business Go?

This is the essence of your story. Every industry is competitive, and small businesses don't last if they don't compete effectively. Long-standing businesses, like those run by the second or third or even fourth generation, must adapt and change to stay alive. What makes this one a winner? Location? Long hours? Good service? Unusual merchandise? Knowledgeable employees? Low prices? Reliable maintenance and repairs? Helpful website? Other Internet presence? Owners and customers may have different views on this; use both.

Customer Quote Near Top

It's important, as stated above, to inform your audience that this isn't just a puff piece conceived by a clever PR person. No, this is genuine journalism. A good way to convey that is to place at least one customer quote high in your story, very high, possibly in the lede. Quotes are always golden in business stories, and this one nicely ruptures the one-source impression that most small-business stories radiate. If the customer has more to say than you can use at this strategic moment, feel free to return to him or her later in the story. It's not wrong to separate a source's quotes, assuming they help you make different points at different places in your story.

Subordinate the History

Again, a chronology is not a news story, no matter how fascinating or remarkable it may be. A good little company undoubtedly has a story behind it, and the owner may well volunteer it even if you don't ask. But when it comes to writing your story, remember that you've got a point to make, a message to attract your audience, so weave the history into that overriding purpose rather than letting it drive or simply bog down your story.

The small business profile can be one of the most enjoyable, even fascinating, stories a business journalist may undertake. It gets you out of the newsroom. You meet lively, creative, engaging people. Your reporting offers creative opportunity for both text and pictures. The challenge is to make it newsworthy and dispassionate, with customer quotes that help to achieve a modicum of balance.

Questions for Discussion

1 To cover a small, service business (say, a software developer, an event planner or a real estate broker) that operates only in an unremarkable office, how could you make the story more visual?
2 If you're doing the story in video, and you find that the owner of your chosen small business is inarticulate, or perhaps speaks with a thick accent, how would you overcome that drawback?
3 When might it be appropriate to include more than one firm in your small-business story?

12 The Trend Story

This story is fun to formulate, to report, and to write. Yet it's a challenge. It requires imagination and multiple interviews or examples. But in the end it's very satisfying, because it's entirely yours, not the government's, not a company's. It can describe either a business trend or a consumer trend, such as increasing patronage of credit unions in the wake of recent bank blemishes. It needs numbers, of course. The credit union story, for instance, would be confirmed by rising deposits in credit unions.

Preparing for the Story

The first challenge, of course, is to identify a trend, and the best way to do that is to keep your eyes open. In your travels, and in your news consumption, observe what people and businesses are doing. If something strikes you as new or different, you may be on to something. It's been said that one event is a novelty, two are an anomaly, and three make a trend. That's not far off, for if you can spot three similar incidences, there probably are more.

On occasion one of my journalism students looking for a trend has simply taken a walk. One noticed, in a Chicago neighborhood, a number of suburban auto stickers, indicating that small shops there had an unexpectedly broad appeal. He confirmed it with the shops and some customers. Good story! Another student reporter, walking a redeveloping former commercial area near Chicago's downtown Loop, saw a number of new apartment buildings but no coffee shops, convenience stores, taverns or other attributes of a true neighborhood. Bingo! He interviewed local residents, who said they missed a congenial neighborhood feeling.

The moral is, of course, to explore surprises that you notice. If you're new on your beat, what's a surprise may not be obvious. Is this really different, or is this simply the way this industry operates? Answering that usually requires some reporting. Ask an analyst, ask a homeowner, ask a shopper on the street. You may not strike gold on your first try, but that's journalism, *good* journalism. Lots of story ideas don't work out, and testing them is the road to good stories.

Consult Experts

Local interviewing may suffice to prove your trend, as in the examples above, but, particularly with a business (rather than consumer) trend, you'll probably benefit by talking to outside experts. To fortify your several examples of local manufacturers' reducing foreign outsourcing in favor of more on-site production, get a comment from a securities analyst who covers manufacturers like 3M or Borg Warner or General Electric. Or ask a university press office to recommend an economist who follows manufacturing or the gross domestic product (GDP).

Watch National Trends

It's OK to localize a national trend that's been reported by a TV network or a national publication. But it's not sufficient to just recite the national story and add a local interview or two. Credible, newsworthy localization requires local statistics, local consumers and businesses, and local experts, though it will be ethically appropriate to acknowledge the original, national story in some fashion.

Structuring the Story

Like the small business story, there's an opportunity here to be creative, so long as you adhere to your objective of drawing readers to your story and engaging their attention to read on. So your lede may be anecdotal, or an illustrative quote, but resist the temptation to start by writing, "Time was when people kept their savings under their pillow…" or some such stage-setting. Too trite. Too wordy. Too slow. Get to the point. You have only a couple of seconds to persuade your audience that you have something worthwhile to say.

Quotes and Numbers

As in all business stories, these are essential. When a businessman tells you, "we're selling twice as much to Asia," get specifics: Is he comparing with last year, or when? What countries are buying the most? What products are selling best? What proportion of total sales are to Asia? And, of course, why? Economists or the government (primarily the Department of Commerce, the Department of Labor or the Census Bureau) may provide supportive statistics.

The "However" Graf

In identifying almost any trend, you'll encounter exceptions: people who still do things the old way, or businesses that think some new-fangled innovation is crazy. You want them in your story, too. Otherwise it may appear naive, implying that the whole world is moving in a new direction. It never is, and good journalism recognizes that. And again, don't attach this "to be sure" or "however" paragraph to the end of your story; it belongs somewhere in the body, then you can return to the quotes and illustrations of your trend.

Conclusion: Don't Bury a Great Quote

Editors will differ on how to conclude your trend story, or any feature story for that matter. The artists want a conclusion of some sort, perhaps a great quote that nicely wraps up your idea. The problem is that these days many readers won't stay with your story until the end, particularly if it's online. A better strategy is to get your best stuff up high in the story, relegating lesser quotes and data to the nether regions. In particular, don't bury a nifty quote, saving it to the end. The higher it is, the more people will read it. Show them what a great reporter you are, eliciting such a fine expression of your story idea.

Questions for Discussion

1 If a local trend you detect is substantiated by interviews and examples but isn't corroborated by national or regional sales figures or other data, is it still a trend story? How?
2 If your interviews and examples are inconsistent or even contradictory, how might you still fashion a trend story out of them?
3 If you set out to illustrate a national trend with local interviews and examples, and they run contrary to the national trend, have you lost your story? Why or why not?

13 The Consumer Story

Does this seem obvious? Consumer spending is two-thirds of our gross domestic product (GDP). So we consumers, collectively, are a huge, influential part of the American economy. If we don't buy a product, no matter how nifty, it's toast. But to some folks (even some business reporters) who take a macro view of economics, consumers are merely a reflection of the really important factors, actions by companies and governments. Not so. Even machine tools and heavy machinery manufacturing depend on consumers indirectly, for what's being built (or imported) needs a market, and eventually *we* are that market. In the end, consumers decide.

As shown earlier, consumer quotes can brighten and humanize the small-business story and the economic indicator story. In fact, *any* business story. So this chapter's focus on the consumer story shouldn't be taken to imply that consumer angles are best confined to stories that are exclusively consumer-centric. We should recognize that there's some overlap here with the consumer trend stories discussed in the preceding chapter, but the consumer story typically doesn't rise to the level of a trend story, either because it's based on fewer interviews or doesn't have any statistical support. In any event, the consumer story is distinctive and important enough to warrant this separate mention.

For a business reporter, there's a particular satisfaction in originating and reporting a consumer story. You're going directly to the foundation of the economy, with no PR people or other intermediaries or guidance directing you. This is real, this is genuine. And consumers say the funniest things! Recording their comments is definitely helpful, but many states forbid recording a conversation unless both sides agree, so be sure to tell (or show) your interviewees if you're recording and give them a moment to object. If you're doing video interviews, get a colleague to handle the camera (on a tripod!) so you can concentrate on your interviewing, and vary the camera angles and backgrounds so people don't pop in and out of the same background in your edited story.

In fact, on-the-street interviews may constitute an entire consumer story. Focus on an issue that affects everybody (like the cost of living, or saving vs. spending, or whether to buy a car), that you can present in a simple, pithy question, and that can, at least ideally, be answered readily and briefly. You may want to refer to a recent report or study about consumer spending, or a contemplated tax increase, or adverse weather, or anything else that's likely to affect consumer behavior or taste.

Investments, Anyone?

If your question concerns consumer saving for vacations or college educations or retirement, you'll need more time than the typical on-the-street interview allows, and you'll also need some knowledge of investing. So let's consider the likely possibilities.

Bank Accounts

This sounds like a prosaic no-brainer, especially in times of low interest rates like the years following the Great Recession of 2007–2009, when the Federal Reserve Board (the odd name for the United States central bank), which controls short-term interest rates, was trying to encourage borrowing to stimulate the economy. (N.B.: the Fed's "open-market" operations, the buying and selling of U.S. Treasury bonds to control interest rates, are its way of exercising the nation's **monetary policy**, not to be confused with **fiscal policy**, which is the management of the national budget and the borrowing by the Treasury Department to finance the national deficit, controlled by Congress and the President.) But bank accounts are always attractive because they're insured by the Federal Deposit Insurance Corporation up to $250,000. And in more normal times a bank account may earn interest that exceeds inflation. The best way for a consumer to maximize the interest return on a bank account is to put at least part of the money into a time deposit, usually called a certificate of deposit. If you agree to leave your money untouched for six months or a year or perhaps even three or four years, the bank will pay you more interest and probably add the annual interest to your principal, i.e., compound the interest. That's the time-honored and safest way of making your money work for you.

A bank account is considered the most conservative mode of saving. There are lots of riskier ways.

Stocks and Mutual Funds

The **stock market** is glamorous, even alluring, because picking the right stock can bring outsize rewards, sometimes quickly if you believe the myths.

But if you pick wrong, the loss can be equally stunning. So the risk of buying stock is always significant.

What's a stock? A stock is a tiny share of ownership in a big corporation (it must be incorporated in order to have shares) like General Motors or General Electric. Depending on the company, owning shares may entitle the investor to an annual dividend, perhaps as much as two percent or three percent of the price of the stock. But beware: some very successful companies like Microsoft pay no annual dividend at all. The only possible profit for a shareholder in such a company is appreciation of the stock. That may work, but then again, it may not. An investment in stock is termed an "equity" investment.

A particular, and popular, variety of equity investment is a **real estate investment trust**, or REIT, which is the stock of a company that owns and manages a large number of real estate properties. They may be residential or commercial, but they're always specialized, such as apartment buildings, or health care properties, or retirement communities, or factories and warehouses. REITs have a unique tax advantage accorded by Congress: they pay little or no federal income tax so long as they distribute at least 90 percent of their profits to their shareholders. For an investor, if the REIT is well managed and profitable, that typically means a generous dividend, perhaps 5 percent or more, and that means in turn that the stock will retain its value, i.e., less downside risk. And there's always the possibility that the stock will appreciate, though perhaps less than the wider market. In other words, a REIT is a conservative way to invest in the stock market, ideal for someone who wants dividend income and below-average risk.

Another popular way to invest in the stock market, also intended to mitigate risk, is to buy shares in a **mutual fund**, which is a professionally managed pool of money that buys lots of different stocks, typically in some defined category like high tech or real estate or Asia or large "high-cap" stocks. This relieves the investor of the need to "follow the market" and make his or her own investment decisions, and many people appreciate that sense of comfort.

Because the managers of mutual funds charge a fee for their expert services, a low-cost alternative pioneered a few decades ago by a mutual-fund company called Vanguard is the **index fund**. It's not actively managed so fees are infinitesimal, only a fraction of 1 percent of your investment. The fund's money is invested in the stocks in a market index, like the Standard & Poor's 500 Stock Index, so the fund moves with the index. The managers of mutual funds, or all professional asset managers for that matter, strive to "beat the market," which typically refers to the S&P 500, but over time most of them fail to do so. Yet, in fair weather and foul, they always charge 1 percent or more of the value of the assets they manage, which is very nice

86   *The Consumer Story*

for them but not so nice for their investors except in those occasional years when they do in fact "beat the market." These days a number of mutual-fund companies offer low-fee index funds. A variety of index fund is an **exchange traded fund**, or ETF. An ETF is itself a corporation with publicly traded shares. ETF shares, like the shares of any publicly owned company, are marketable, meaning that the ETF investor may readily sell the shares on a stock market, not dependent on the readiness of the fund manager to redeem shares, which is the usual way an investor in an ordinary mutual fund "cashes out."

Bonds

A bond is a safer, more conservative investment than a stock. The issuer of a bond (the borrower, in effect), which may be a company or a government agency, promises to pay interest at a rate higher than most stock dividend returns, and at maturity, which may be 10 or 20 or even 30 years hence, repay the full amount invested. So if the investor wants to put some money away for a specific and substantial future expense, like college tuition bills, a bond might be an appropriate investment. Moreover, a bond, like a stock, may be sold at any time if cash is needed or a better opportunity arises, and the market price typically varies only slightly (that happens with variations in interest rates, meaning that when rates rise, the value of the bond drops a bit), so the principal invested in a bond is predictably secure during the entire life of the bond. Nice. On Wall Street bonds are called "fixed-income" investments.

Bonds issued by states or cities or special districts like school districts are called municipal bonds. They offer lower interest rates than corporate bonds, because the interest is exempt from income taxation by the federal government. So they're called "tax-exempts." Such bonds are particularly attractive to wealthy taxpayers in the upper income-tax brackets.

An investor seeking the safety of bonds may consider a bond mutual fund, which, like a stock mutual fund, is a pool of professionally managed money invested in a large number of bonds, again to abate risk.

So, this has been a long a rather long primer about investments in this consumer-story discussion, but it's necessary if you plunge into a story about personal income or disposable income or saving. And it's just good stuff for anyone who has an interest in money to know. Helpful for management of personal finances, too. In the next chapter we'll look at a kind of very sophisticated investment, derivative securities, which aren't likely to be of interest to most consumers, but a financial journalist needs to know about them, too.

Whenever you're afflicted by newsroom claustrophobia or bottom-burn or telephone ear, conjure up a consumer story and get out on the street. Good for a journalist's morale, good for journalism!

Questions for Discussion

1 Would it be ethical, and manageable, to interview only *some* consumers, e.g., only women, or only tall people, or only out-of-town visitors? What would be an appropriate question?
2 Are there advantages, or disadvantages, to interviewing on the street with only a note pad, or with only an audio recorder, or with only a video camera? Which would you prefer? Why?
3 Is there any subject so insignificant, or so frivolous, that you'd rule it out as a subject for a consumer story? Why, or why not? (Hint: there's a story in everything!)

14 The Derivatives Story

American Ingenuity at Work

What's a derivative? It used to be obscure, but it became prominent, perhaps notorious, as the root cause of the Great Recession of 2007–2009. More properly, it's a derivative security, which means that its value is based on the value of something else.

Futures

The best illustration is the very first derivative security, the **futures contract**, created by the Chicago Board of Trade in the mid-nineteenth century. In those days farmers trucked their crop, such as corn, into the city after harvesting it in the fall, and sold it to millers, bakers, processors and other users through the Board of Trade. But sometimes during harvest season there was an oversupply, indeed a glut, so that prices dropped precipitously. This robbed farmers of the true value of their work, in extreme cases causing such despair that they actually dumped their corn into the Chicago River in protest. But at other times of year the supply of corn was meager, so buyers bid the price up.

What to do about this imbalance, this inordinate risk in the marketplace? Members of the Board of Trade came up with the futures contract, beneficial to both farmers and users of corn. It worked like this: instead of bargaining for a cash price and immediate delivery, seller and buyer would agree on a contract, an agreement, by which the seller promised to deliver a certain amount of corn to the buyer at a specified place and specified future date, at a price determined by bargaining or negotiation, today. In other words, the seller (the farmer) could "lock in" a price for his crop months before he harvested it, assuring him a fair return for his labors, and the buyer (the miller, the processor) could lock in an assured supply at a certain time at a price that he, too, considered fair. Both parties obtained a comforting assurance that obviated future risk and anxiety. In other words, they hedged. The price of each contract was determined by the sometimes-tumultuous open-outcry trading that made the Board of Trade famous.

Sometimes the benefit of a futures contract was most apparent when the corn harvest was unexpectedly good or bad. For instance, if a farmer negotiated a futures contract for his crop, and there was a bountiful harvest that year that augmented supply and drove the cash or current price of corn down, the farmer still got the price he agreed to in the spring. On the other hand, if a drought impaired the harvest and drove the cash price up, the corn processor still paid just the price he had negotiated earlier.

Many of the traders in the huge octagonal pits at the Board of Trade were brokers who represented farmers or buyers, the hedgers, but they were quickly augmented by speculators trading for their own pockets. The speculators were neither suppliers nor users of corn. They sought to make a living by buying and selling frequently to gain pennies on each contract, always making sure that they sold any contract before the settlement date so that they didn't have to deliver thousands of bushels of corn, nor would those bushels be dumped at their house. The speculators often took the other side of a hedger's trade. In other words, if a farmer sought to sell his crop, locking in a price for the fall, a speculator might take that deal, hoping that the price of corn would rise at some point, enabling him to sell the contract at a profit. While the hedger strove to reduce risk, the speculator was keen to assume risk, for without it there was no gain possible. In effect, they counterbalanced each other.

The speculators, self-centered though they were, brought a benefit to the market by their constant buying and selling: greater liquidity. Liquidity was essential to the market. It represented an assurance that any buyer or seller could make a deal whenever the market was open. And that assurance attracted even more buyers and sellers.

The derivative securities contract was born.

The Chicago Board of Trade later created futures contracts for other commodities: soybeans, wheat, rice and more. Imitation being the sincerest form of flattery, other Chicago entrepreneurs, veterans of the Board of Trade, later launched a new exchange called the Butter and Egg Board, which grew into the Chicago Mercantile Exchange. It traded other agricultural products, such as live cattle and frozen pork bellies, a colorful name given to sides of bacon. In time other futures exchanges were created, in New York, to trade metals, crude oil and other petroleum products.

These exchanges on which these futures contracts are traded, like stock exchanges, are registered with and supervised by a government regulator, in this case the Commodity Futures Trading Commission rather than the Securities and Exchange Commission. And like the stock exchanges they used to operate in open pits through open-outcry trading, but they, too, have given way to trading "on the screen." So both hedgers and speculators may be located anywhere in the world, at a computer, striving either to abate risk or take it on.

Financial Futures

In the last half of the twentieth century, the Chicago Mercantile Exchange launched an historic innovation: futures contracts on financial products, such as government bonds, stock indexes and currencies. They worked the same way as corn futures: the buyer and seller (or their brokers) could bargain in noisy open-outcry pits to agree on a price for the delivery of a bond at a specified future date. If there was no tangible product to be delivered, such as a contract on the Standard & Poor's 500 Stock Index, when the contract matured it was simply settled in money. Like commodities futures, these financial contracts alleviated risk, providing assurance and certainty, not only for actual users of these products like banks and other financial businesses, but for any company or individual engaged in business or investing, all hedgers. And of course, they, too, attracted speculators who added to the frenzy, but also to the essential liquidity, of the trading pits.

Options

Chicago innovators weren't done. In 1973 members of the Board of Trade established in one room of their building on LaSalle Street an entirely new exchange, the Chicago Board Options Exchange, to trade another derivative security: an **option on stocks**. This option wasn't brand new. Options had been traded privately for decades, often between securities firms. In fact there were two options, **puts** and **calls**. The holder of a put option had the right to *sell* a certain stock at a certain price for a period of months into the future. The holder of a call option had the right to *buy* a certain stock at a certain price for a specified time. The Chicago innovation was to form an exchange that would trade certain, listed options created by the exchange, on specific stocks for specified periods of time. The exchange set the terms, except the price of the option. If the holder of a call option on 100 shares of Boeing at $130 (at or near the current market price of the stock) saw the market price rise to $140, he could exercise his option, acquire the shares and immediately sell them for a $10 profit (less the dollar or two paid for the option, called the premium). On the other hand, if the holder of a put option at $130 saw Boeing stock decline to $120, he could go into the market, buy 100 shares of Boeing for $120 and promptly exercise his option, selling the shares for $130, turning a similar profit.

Derivatives Agonistes

So how did derivatives spark the Great Recession? It wasn't the futures or options traded on exchanges. As noted in Chapter 1, the problem was other derivative securities, in this case bonds, created by Wall Street firms and government-chartered mortgage companies Fannie Mae and Freddie Mac. They took advantage of rising real estate prices in the early 2000s, a rise fueled by hopeful home buyers and also by speculators who began rapidly buying and selling homes, called "flipping" them, at a profit.

Some of the demand was stimulated by home-loan lenders or mortgage companies that lowered the usual standards of mortgage loans. Traditionally, a mortgage loan had called for a minimum down payment of 20 percent or even 30 percent and an interest rate of about 6 percent, and had limited the monthly payments (principal and interest on the loan, plus insurance and property taxes) to 30 percent of the buyer's income. As home prices rose, some less-principled lenders and mortgage brokers lowered the standards, offering mortgage loans at low down payments of 5 percent or even less, and charging "teaser" rates of 1 or 2 percent with an automatic escalation after a year or two to 8 or 10 percent.

Don't worry, the buyers were told, your home will appreciate in value during that time so that you can refinance, meaning obtain a larger loan based on the greater value of your home, and again obtain a low interest rate that will make your monthly payments manageable. Sometimes that worked. But the housing bubble burst and prices collapsed in 2007–2008, leaving many home buyers stranded, holding mortgages they couldn't pay as the rates of their loans escalated while their unrealistic home values went south, so they defaulted. Many of them just moved out and delivered their keys to the bank.

Problem Derivatives

However, in the meantime, Wall Street financial firms and the government-created (but now privatized) mortgage companies Fannie Mae and Freddie Mac had created new forms of derivative securities. They were long-term bonds with thousands of the high-risk, non-standard mortgages as collateral, supposedly assuring the buyers of the bonds that in the event of default by the issuers of the bonds that the value of the underlying homes would assure total repayment. The bonds were called **mortgage-backed securities**, or **MBS**. They were rated AAA, the best, by the ratings firms. They sold so well that Wall Street created a new breed of bonds called **collateralized debt obligations**, or **CDOs**, which were secured by packages of those same mortgage-backed securities.

As the buyers of homes subject to the flimsy mortgage loans defaulted in 2007 and 2008, the bonds secured by those mortgages also went into default, and then the insurers of those bonds, the companies that guaranteed payment to the bond investors in the event of default, also defaulted. Two major securities firms, Lehman Bros. and Bear Stearns, failed, and others were at risk. So the government stepped in to prevent a catastrophic collapse of the financial system and perhaps the entire U.S. economy. At the request of the Treasury and the Federal Reserve Board, Congress provided $787 million to buy up defaulted derivative securities and to bail out two tottering giants, General Motors and Citigroup. The Federal Reserve lowered short-term interest rates to near zero and launched a massive "quantitative easing," an unprecedented, continuing purchase of billions of dollars of Treasury bonds. All these programs were designed to forestall further corporate collapses, to pump money into the economy, and to encourage banks to make loans. Fortunately for the economy and the country, it worked.

Derivative securities got a very bad name. Yes, very bad indeed. When Congress got down to writing restrictive legislation designed to impose "never again" on the financial industry, "derivatives" were on every member's tongue.

However, Congress wasn't aiming at exchange-traded futures and options. Already regulated by the Commodity Futures Trading Commission, they were untainted by the Great Recession. But for a reporter covering those exchanges, it's important to know the difference between the derivatives that almost brought down the U.S. economy in the Great Recession, and those that didn't. The listed derivatives are out in the open and fair game, for hedgers, for speculators, and for the press.

The Stories

Because the mainstream financial press will cover the broad trends in the daily exchange trading of both agricultural and financial futures, it's incumbent on beginning reporters to be imaginative, to look for niches and novelties that provide opportunities for fresh, original reporting.

The Traders

The times they are a-changing. Most trading pits are now deserted. Sadly, the colorful open-outcry spectacle is nearly extinct. Most derivatives trading has moved to "the screen." But this tectonic shift creates new story possibilities: the new traders. No longer need serious traders pay six figures for an exchange membership and stand for hours in a trading pit, signaling with their hands and yelling at the top of their lungs. They can be anywhere. They can be part-time. They can continue to carry on their other work. They can be young. And they can be women, whose slight stature was rarely seen in the open-outcry pits, definitely a man's world. Not everyone who trades derivatives does it profitably; many fall by the wayside after taking some losses. But if any of these atypical traders has a hot hand, and will provide enough numbers to demonstrate it, that's a story, a fun story.

There's also a dark side to this move from pit to screen: some accomplished open-outcry traders couldn't make the transition, or didn't want to. They missed the camaraderie and comfort of their success in the pit. No longer could they see the familiar faces they had confidence in that they were used to dealing with. Sitting in front of a computer for hours was a totally different experience, a different world. And, although there are classes in screen trading, older traders in particular found the new world forbidding. So what's become of these displaced persons? One resourceful student reporter found that a number of Chicago traders had taken an unlikely turn, to teaching. A nifty story!

The Anomaly

Although prices of futures of most agricultural commodities, and of most financial instruments, generally move together, either up or down or sideways, there are often exceptions that move in the opposite direction. The sharp decline in the price of oil starting in mid-2014 called attention to the fact that most commodities had been trending downward for some time. However, in early 2015 a few were bucking the trend. They were rising. There had to be a reason, and one such anomalous move made a story.

The VIX

This is the Volatility Index, a clever product created by the Chicago Board Options Exchange. It measures the changes in prices of the CBOE's SPX contract, the Standard & Poor's 500 Stock Index. A high reading, perhaps in the 50s or 60s, is interpreted to predict that coming trading in those stocks will gyrate or move sharply in one direction or the other, while comparatively low readings, say, in the 20s, suggests more placid trading ahead in those same stocks. The VIX can be of interest almost any time, when it's high, when it's low, when it's moving or not. Ask some brokers or securities analysts why the VIX is doing what it's doing, or why it's not doing something else. They'll know, and you'll have a story.

Exchange Operations

Especially for news organizations in cities like Chicago and New York where open-outcry derivatives trading once thrived, the move to computers breeds other story possibilities.

Lost Jobs

Those exchanges once required hundreds of people on the trading floor, some of them employed by the exchange itself, to report the prices of trades, for instance, but most of them in the employ of trading firms or commodity buyers like producers of breakfast cereals or vegetable oils—traders, phone clerks, floor runners and so forth. Many of those jobs are already gone, but the shrinkage continues, and reverberations are felt outside the exchanges, in neighborhood restaurants, bars, shops, bank branches and other service providers like barbers and travel agents. Assessing and relating this somber impact is definitely newsworthy.

What Survives?

Open-outcry remnants persist. They're curiosities. The Chicago Board Options Exchange continues open-outcry trading in its important SPX contract. At the Chicago Board of Trade open-outcry is still noisy and vigorous in trading options on commodity futures contracts (yes, options on futures), which traders say doesn't work well on the screen. The busiest, most boisterous pit at the Chicago Mercantile Exchange is for Eurodollar futures. (Eurodollars are U.S. dollars held in foreign banks.) It's worth exploring the reasons why, and asking whether the trading floors would have any *raison d'être* without these islands of frenzied activity.

Recycling the Floor

A trading floor is a unique space. But it's huge and costly to maintain, even if only partly utilized, so what's a cost-conscious management to do? The Chicago Board Options Exchange now takes group tours into the idle pits to reimagine the action that once took place there, and some of the trading floor is being repurposed. Such transitions are newsworthy.

Quarterly Earnings

It's hardly a novel idea to report the quarterly earnings of the derivatives exchanges, for they're big business, but these stories should look for any impact of the historic transition from the pit to the screen. Are compensation expenses reduced? Is trading volume rising? Are any new products taking off? Are new products more readily introduced and tested? (Even if particular products aren't mentioned in the quarterly financial report or press release, trading-volume figures for each product are published separately and may help you frame earnings-day questions for management and securities analysts.)

Questions for Discussion

1. How much explanation or background is needed in a derivatives story for a general-interest publication? For a general business publication?
2. Is it possible to write a conventional pyramid-style, bang-on lede to properly convey the message of a story as complex as a derivatives story? (Try it.)
3. How can an individual screen trader be found for a story?

15 The Agriculture Story

Why agriculture? It's only 1 percent of our gross domestic product, and only 1 percent of our population is farmers. They're out of sight, unless one should have to drive rather than fly for a vacation or a holiday visit to the relatives. Then, of course, we're exposed to mile upon mile of farmlands, magically green and bountiful for many months in the middle of the year, quietly recuperating through the cold, always punctuated by livestock oblivious to the season. But for a business journalist, farming is big, very big, all year 'round. It's a two hundred billion dollar business, by far the largest and most productive in the world. Importantly, it feeds both us and many others in foreign lands, and who can be oblivious to food?

The Agribusiness Story

Science and technology drive this industry. They continuously creates new varieties of seeds that are ever more productive, and pesticides and herbicides that minimize crop losses. They enhance the breeding and productivity of animals. This is why 1 percent of Americans can feed all the rest. But this success also breeds controversies about animal confinement, farm runoff and genetically modified crops. Lots of story possibilities.

Agribusiness starts with research. Like farm yields, it's abundant. Every state university college of agriculture revolves around research, traditionally focused on the state's own agriculture, but nowadays typically reaching well beyond it. So the University of Illinois College of Agricultural, Consumer and Environmental Sciences, in the midst of the Illinois prairie at Urbana, boasts 250 scientists seeking to enhance production of corn, soybeans, beef, pork and poultry, while also exploring an immense portfolio of broader inquiries such as plant, animal and microbial genomes, biofuels (think ethanol), farm financial performance, human nutrition, protection of natural and human resources (call it agricultural sustainability), even aquaculture and Great Lakes sustainable coastal development.

The University of California's College of Agricultural and Environmental Sciences at Davis, which bills itself as "the #1 college of its kind in the world," operates an Agricultural Experiment Station that, in conjunction with the University's Berkeley and Riverside campuses, boasts 750 scientists conducting 1,300 research projects aiming to improve fruits, vegetables, livestock, wines, pollination and honey, and marine foods; to combat pests (notably that mean glassy-winged sharpshooter); and to tackle larger challenges such as the conservation of natural resources, the safety and health of the food supply and maintaining an economically viable and environmentally sustainable agricultural production system.

Other farm research and development is conducted relentlessly by the giant companies that produce ever-better seeds, fertilizers, machines and farm management tools, the Monsantos and DuPonts and Deeres of the industrial world. Their quarterly and annual reports, while couched in the traditional language of revenues and profits, are fascinating, based on each company's remarkable and continuing contributions to the most progressive and productive agriculture in the world. Monsanto, for instance, years ago created an effective herbicide called Roundup that dominates the world market and now gives rise to a steady flow of new Roundup variations and "Roundup-Ready" seeds that flourish even in the presence of the herbicide. Deere provides access to databases that assist farmers in planning and managing their crops, and installs Global Positioning Systems in its tractors and other machines that assure precise, efficient field operations with no square foot of soil missed or repeated.

The publicly held agribusinesses all had humble, rural origins. The blacksmith John Deere, for instance, invented the self-scouring steel plow in the 1830s. Today such businesses represent the strength and durability of American agriculture.

As mentioned above, it's the scientific advancements that give rise to controversy, sometimes vigorous protests, about certain aspects of American agriculture—the Genetically Modified Organisms, the crowded livestock pens, and the inevitable runoff from feedlots into rivers and lakes, our sources of fresh water. Environmental organizations provide an endless supply of criticisms and complaints, even though mobilizing public opinion, given the evident consumer benefits of efficient, scientific agriculture, is always a tough sell. But is it a story? Of course it is.

The Farmer Story

Perhaps because so few Americans choose farming, and because they are so vitally important to the rest of us, there's a certain fascination about those who work the land. Farmers are simply woven into the romance of America, our history and our literature. So it's newsworthy, and always enjoyable, to take an occasional look into how today's college-educated farmer juggles chemistry and agronomy and genetics and capital investment and taxes and futures and who knows what else, utilizing them all to turn a profit year after year, enabling him (and occasionally her) to stay on the land. For they all were born and raised there. No city dweller chooses to buy farmland (for perhaps $10,000 an acre) or even rent it to become a professional farmer. (For occasional, organic exceptions, see below.) Of course, this steadfast attachment to the land merely enhances the farmer mystique.

So how to write a business story, a story that capitalizes on the myth without becoming entranced by it?

Like all solid business stories, this one requires numbers. Some, the macroeconomics, are readily available from the U.S. Department of Agriculture, other federal agencies, perhaps state agriculture departments, real estate agents or farm brokers, and other sources. At the other end of agriculture, the retail prices of what farmers produce are readily available. But that leaves a middle ground, territory that only the farmer himself can cover for you: his own costs—seed, fertilizer, machinery maintenance and occasional purchases, upkeep of barns and other real estate improvements, perhaps labor, insurance, taxes, and so on—set against his crop and livestock revenues and any federal payments such as crop insurance. It will be unlikely, if not impossible, to find a farmer who will provide such detailed disclosures to a reporter. After all, they don't have to tell you anything. And it's all quite private.

However, don't give up. In lieu of dollar figures, your farmer might disclose percentage gains or losses, ups or downs, measuring one season against its predecessor, or his best or worst recent year, either for a certain crop or the entire farm. He might also divulge the purchase price of some additional acreage (which helps spread his total costs over a bigger harvest) or a new tractor or combine—big, six-figure investments. Although such occasional numbers are hardly comprehensive, they help convey the tone and substance of a business story.

Pictures are a must for the farmer story, which means, at least for field crops in the North, skip the winter. Use that quiet season to identify your farmer, perhaps through the state Farm Bureau or other agriculture organization, and arrange your visit. Spring, summer and fall are always fine. Farmers are in motion then, so schedule your visit for a day when your subject is at his photogenic best, ideally on his tractor or other field machine.

The best farm stories, like other stories, will convey a message, a message that can be summarized in the lede and then buttressed by the specifics below. Traditional pyramid style, in other words. It may be tempting to settle for a featurish "here's a local farmer," but don't. As always, ask your subject what's new, what's different this year from last and what his business's toughest challenges or uncertainties are. The answers should provide your message and your lede.

One endlessly fascinating story these days is about the children of farmers—why they do or don't decide to stay on the land, to follow their forefathers. The commitment to farm is great, and the temptations to leave are many, especially because a college education is required either way. There's just no way a farm youngster, no matter how bright, even with the prospect of inheriting free land, can nowadays just "pick up" farming with all its modern demands and nuances, from finance and futures and taxes and return on investment to the sciences of seeds, fertilizers, soils and weather.

Farming, as traditional and conventional as it may appear on a drive through the country, is constantly changing, improving, modernizing, like any competitive business. Even if you're not in a position to follow agriculture closely, your state has farmers and immigrant farm labor and probably a school of agriculture, so touching base occasionally with agriculture sources, in companies, the university or agriculture associations such as the Farm Bureau, will sometimes lead you to a story about a change in farming or food that's worth covering.

Urban Agriculture

Does that sound like an oxymoron? Well, perhaps it should be in quotation marks, but it's still the best way to describe a genre of news about the growing practice of raising crops and chickens or other livestock (even alpacas!) in the city, and the widespread preference for organic foods. Even if urban farming enterprises often aren't for-profit, there are dollar costs and benefits to write about. How much does the feed for three or four chickens cost, and how much does the family save in supermarket purchases of eggs? Think also: community vegetable gardens on stray bits of idle land, aquaponic cultivation and small organic farms on the city's outskirts. Some such farms are built on a financial base that's both modern and historic: pre-season sales of "shares," not true equity ownership but shares of the season's produce to be delivered weekly to the investors' doors. And don't ignore farmers markets, which sometimes are an outlet for those local organic farms but more likely are supplied by fruit and vegetable farmers 100 or 200 miles away who get up at 2 in the morning to set up shop in the city before rush hour—in other words, a precious chance for farm and city folks to get acquainted with each other. Prices help make all these city stories.

Then there are small ventures that materialize to support urban farms, such as the supplier of chicken feed who makes home deliveries. On the consumer side, which always has broad appeal, there are good stories that grow out of both farm megatrends and local urban agriculture, such as the growing (no pun intended) preference for organic foods.

It's an understatement to say that urban journalism isn't exactly geared to dig agriculture for newsworthy business stories of broad interest. But they're ripe for the picking.

Questions for Discussion

1 How should a reporter develop data and quotes that lend broader significance to an agriculture business story based on local events or people?
2 Are consumers essential to a farm business story?
3 How do you distinguish a traditional family farm from a corporate farm?

16 The Sports Business Story

Because there's such huge interest in sports—at all levels—there's a market for stories about the business of sports, too. But they're not nearly as obvious, nor are the necessary numbers as available, as in stories about the sports themselves. Lots of data there! Enterprise reporting is required, and it's rewarding. Following are some angles worth pursuing.

The Athlete Story

There will never be a lack of interest in the players themselves, those "in the arena," as celebrated by Teddy Roosevelt. Of course the pro sports writers are incessantly covering, interpreting and advising all the big-time athletes. Or are they? In fact, there are many athletes who labor with little love from the press: minor leaguers, women, participants in disfavored sports such as boxing or "Olympics-only" sports such as speed skating, and most amateurs (excepting the big-time college football and basketball players). So if one such athlete is willing to reveal salary and talk about the economic basis of his or her sport, that's the making of an unusual but engaging sports business story

The Fan Story

On the perimeter of the arena, there are the fans. That's most of us. So, like any consumer story, there's a built-in audience for a sports business story that focuses on us. One angle, always good, is to examine today's cost of attending a ball game, including public transportation or parking, hot dogs and drinks, maybe a T-shirt or other souvenir—for a couple, or better, for a family. When the cost for a couple exceeds $100, or perhaps $200 for a family, that's a story worth telling—and remarking about. Will businesses' season tickets, skyboxes, box seats and other preferential seating eventually crowd out the individual fan, or relegate him to the rafters?

Another good fan story is to examine how sports teams are trying to market their product to us. They often employ sports-marketing firms, the folks who analyze ticket-buying and seating patterns, souvenir and snack sales, even the use of restrooms, supplemented with polls and surveys to detect fan likes and dislikes, why we do what we do, or don't do, in response to team records, ballpark facilities and team advertising. Such a firm is likely to be quite receptive to a story about it and the great job it's doing for its clients. What's the secret of its success? Are its revenues rising this year? By what percentage? Why can we assume that this is a success story? Because a firm that fails won't be around for long.

Sports marketing isn't limited to the big leagues or the big cities. Every minor league baseball team is a marketing operation. Their players are under contract to the parent major league team, just on loan to the minor league team. So the team's marketing director, who might even be the owner of the minor league franchise or one of his partners, is tasked with creating advertising and attractions such as between-innings horseplay and giveaways that will appeal to the public, even folks who don't much care for baseball but who might enjoy the relaxed atmosphere and the laughs of a low-cost outing with family or friends. A good business story will describe (and photograph) what works and what doesn't, what ticket prices are attractive to the public, the attendance needed for a profitable game and a profitable season, what salaries the team can afford to pay its players, whether the team paid a dividend to its shareholders last year, and whether the stock is appreciating, if any sales have taken place.

The Public-Company Story

Although most professional sports teams are privately owned and publish no financial reports (they would make juicy reading!), there are a few publicly held sports businesses. One is World Wrestling Entertainment Inc. (if one can consider pro wrestling a sport), and another is the prominent retail chain Dick's Sporting Goods Inc. The success of such businesses depends to a considerable extent on fan adulation of sports heroes, and, at least in Dick's case, on public participation in sports and exercise of all kinds. So, once again, there's a wide potential audience, and quarterly earnings reports once again provide considerable grist for the business journalist's mill.

The Private Sports-Dependent Business Story

Lots of smaller enterprises such as ticket resellers (if they're legal), sports bars, T-shirt printers and—would you believe—sports psychologists, need successful professional or college sports to feed off. Every town has them. Depending, as always, on obtaining some numbers from them, such businesses can make good reading. Since they're likely to face considerable competition, how do they emerge from the pack? Price? Location? Website?

The College Sports Story

We're still talking business here. Coaches' multimillion dollar salaries (far exceeding the university presidents') and athletes' clamoring to be paid already make news. Sometimes the figures are eye-popping. So how does a university, especially a public university created expressly to educate the young people of the state, explain and justify enormous expenditures on sports? More specifically, on just two sports, football and basketball? And what if the players don't graduate, maybe can't? Is it still higher education? Is it a justifiable public expenditure? Taxpayers might be surprised, even appalled, at what's being done in their name. Well worth exploring.

Anything else? Is there more? Of course there is.

All sports, from Little League on up, have expenses, expenses that are escalating to the point that even in Canada some youngsters' families can no longer afford the equipment and rink expense of youth hockey! Another big and growing expense, at least in some areas, is the cost of travel and even professional coaches, as kids' teams play farther and farther afield, and longer and longer schedules. Do these expenses leave some youngsters, and their families, on the sidelines?

Unfortunately, even kids' sports result in injuries that raise questions about insurance and its cost. Yes, there's a dollar sign on everything in sports, and you don't have to be a business reporter to keep your eyes open for a newsworthy tale to tell. How much is your local school board spending on sports-related insurance these days?

Questions for Discussion

1 What numbers might you find, or generate, to write a business story about a team or league whose finances are private?
2 Do local college players lose their scholarships if they're injured and can no longer play? Should they? What are the financial considerations, pro and con?
3 Should sports reporters probe the finances of the teams they cover, or would they offend sources and therefore leave financial stories to the business reporters?

17 The Energy Story

The best energy stories these days may be about efforts to reduce pollution from power generation. Everyone cares about this. Power plants, many still burning coal, are the biggest source of air pollution. That calls for smokestack scrubbers, and, in the long run, nuclear, solar and wind power—all costly. Pollution reduction also means efforts to conserve fuel and power usage, in homes, offices, factories, vehicles, everywhere. Some such efforts must be public, some are private. Of course all the stories need numbers. How much is pollution reduced? How much does it cost? Who pays? What are the expected health benefits?

The Government Pollution-Control Story

There are two aspects of government action to reduce pollution: regulatory, and facilities management.

The Regulatory Story

It's generally acknowledged that solar and wind power are still not economically feasible. To make investing in them profitable, they need tax breaks. For some years the federal government has offered this crucial incentive, but never on a multiyear, predictable basis, which frustrates developers and investors. So, as Congress vacillates, often on an annual basis, investment and construction planning are interrupted, delayed, put on hold. This eternal ambivalence in Washington is a story in itself. The impact on the solar and wind industries is still another story, always worth exploring, especially as to planned local installations. So this is a fine opportunity for a microcosm story, to show the deleterious impact of Washington indecision on the financing, property acquisition, staffing, perhaps subcontracting, and actual construction of a solar or wind energy project.

Another regulatory story is forced reduction of fuel consumption, such as the imposition of mileage standards on the auto industry and direct limits on diesel engine emissions. How industry responds to such limitations may also yield stories, especially when a manufacturer can't measure up, as when truck maker Navistar International Corp. couldn't meet new, well-advertised diesel-emission standards in the early 2000s and so for some time had to buy engines from elsewhere to install in its vehicles. The CEO was fired.

Carbon cap-and-trade limits have long been debated but never adopted in Washington, while California, often a leader in pollution control, went ahead on its own in 2012. (Quebec did so as well, and the two have coordinated their plans.) Under California's plan, the state's Air Resources Board auctions emissions allowances to industrial emitters of greenhouse gases. Allowances are given freely to electric utilities to mitigate costs on customers, but the utilities must use the value of those allowances to benefit the ratepayers. The regulated companies can also meet a small part of their obligations by buying emissions allowances from unregulated companies. In January 2015 Governor Jerry Brown, pushing further ahead, announced in his State-of-the-State address ambitious new goals for 2030: to reduce petroleum usage by half, and to produce half the state's electricity from renewable sources.

As other states, looking to California's example consider cap-and-trade measures, the story possibilities will be abundant.

The Facilities Management Story

Our governments own and operate lots of vehicles and buildings. Sometimes they make efforts to mitigate their own pollution, such as switching to hybrid or liquid-natural-gas buses. The Chicago city government has taken particular pride in planting green roofs on the city hall and other municipal buildings. Such cover is said to reduce heating and cooling bills (and thus emissions), and to return oxygen to the atmosphere. But, as with all government boasts, skeptical coverage is warranted. What do the green roofs cost, and how much is actually saved in operating expenses?

The Industry Pollution-Control Story

Despite the federal stuttering on tax incentives, solar and wind power have advanced, if slowly and unevenly. This progress gives rise notably to stories about commercial and residential solar-panel installations (encouraged by government grants and tax breaks) and the small companies that have emerged to do the work, and stories on local arguments over zoning regulations or permits to bring the massive wind turbines to rural areas. Another wind story is installation of single, proprietary turbines, most likely by public entities or companies to provide their own power. How much do they cost? How long will it take to recover that outlay?

Before we leave private industry, one may question whether the disposal of spent nuclear fuel is a matter of pollution control, but it's certainly environmental, and this seemingly perpetual dilemma is a concern for both nuclear-power companies and government, still wide open since the rejection of the federal government's plan to entomb the remains in Nevada's Yucca Mountain. What to do? Just to remind the public of the continuing conundrum, and whatever dangers it may pose, this is worthy of revisiting from time to time.

Pollution control is sure to be a winning journalistic favorite for decades to come. The stories are newsworthy, and important! But they should go beyond the glowing announcements, following up months and even years later to assess the results.

Questions for Discussion

1 How might a journalist guard against producing only one-sided, purely favorable stories about pollution control efforts, inasmuch as most readers (perhaps excepting those in coal and oil country) are likely to be kindly disposed toward them?
2 Would it be appropriate for media companies to install their own air-pollution measurement devices, as a check on self-congratulatory government announcements of progress?
3 Since all countries need power and need to control pollution, yet handle power generation differently, should journalism do more to report on practices and progress in other countries?

18 The Not-for-Profit Story

Museums, symphony orchestras, theatre and opera companies, aquariums and planetariums have much in common. They inform and enrich our lives. They have big ambitions and big budgets. They depend on donations, some from government but mostly from us, the public. And, though they don't have a bottom line as for-profits do, increasingly they are being run by experienced managers who know how to borrow from the private sector.

What does that mean? It means they try to operate more efficiently, and they seek to enhance public interest, attendance and, of course, contributions. So how does a reporter who's accustomed to addressing earnings and stock prices come to grips with these charitable organizations?

First, what are they, legally? They are not-for-profits whose purpose is educational, religious, charitable, scientific or literary, and thus qualified for recognition by the Internal Revenue Service as tax-exempt under section 501(c)(3) of the Internal Revenue Code. Tax exemptions means two important things: they don't pay taxes, and contributions to them are tax-deductible by the donors. Whenever there's talk in Washington about an across-the-board closing of "tax loopholes," eliminating most deductions, the nation's tax-exempt organizations rise up in solid and loud opposition, fearing that if their donors can't deduct their contributions, they'll dry up.

Next, if you're eyeing a particular not-for-profit for a story about how well it's doing those days, the place to start is the organization's annual return to the Internal Revenue Service. What? A not-for-profit must file a tax return? Yes. But it's different, intended not to calculate its tax, because there is none, but to assure the IRS and the public that the organization is adhering to its stated educational mission. This IRS Form 990 must be available to the public, and many not-for-profits will provide a link to it on their website. GuideStar, itself a not-for-profit, makes Form 990s of many not-for-profits available to subscribing members, and an organization called Public Resource makes an extensive 990 database called Nonprofit Explorer available through ProPublica, the premier not-for-profit news organization.

What can we learn from a Form 990 if there's no income tax? Lots. It's a combination income statement and balance sheet. So it provides revenues, broken down into contributions and earned income like admissions and merchandise sales. Significantly, it tells fundraising costs, with a separate figure for payments to outside fundraisers; generally the most successful fundraising organizations, like WGBH in Boston, for instance, spend the most on fundraising, with extensive inside staffs. And the 990 sets forth expenditures, including total staff compensation and individual compensation for the top-paid employees. The bottom line, the difference between revenue and expense, is called the fund balance, but it's the same as profit or loss in a for-profit corporation. Needless to say, even a not-for-profit has to make a "profit" or at least break even, over time if not every year, or it won't be around for long.

The Great Recession of 2007–2009 threw many not-for-profits for a loop, as donors pulled in their horns to wait it out, and even some major institutions had trouble regaining their footing. For instance, the mighty Art Institute of Chicago, its Form 990s reveal, saw its contributions drop from $79.9 million in its fiscal year ended June 30, 2011 to $62.3 million the next year and further to $51.7 million in 2013, contributing that year to a hefty operating deficit of $16.9 million. For the Art Institute, contributions are its number two revenue source, exceeded only by admissions and other "program service revenues," but they, too, dropped in those two years, from $214.4 million to $160.2 million.

Might a reporter look for a possible story behind such a major swing in an organization's finances? What changes were necessitated? How did they affect the organization's operations, its "mission"? Worth an inquiry.

Displaying an imaginative financial spark, in the winter of 2015 the Art Institute's neighbor in Chicago's Grant Park, the Adler Planetarium, turned to that most modern fundraising strategy, crowdsourcing. It announced a quest for $95,000 to upgrade its "Mission Moon" exhibit about the troubled flight of Apollo 13, led by Chicago-area resident James Lovell. The crowdsourcing partner, IndieGoGo, displayed a running total of the dollars raised and the percentage of the goal achieved. This novel undertaking was definitely worth a story. Of course it needed some financial background, readily obtainable from the Adler's 990s. They revealed that contributions, the planetarium's principal revenue source, were wavering, from $11.7 million in the year ended June 30, 2011, up to $14.1 million the following year, but then sharply down to $8.1 million, triggering an operating deficit of $5.1 million in 2013. Unfortunately, the crowdsourcing effort was not successful.

We should note that Form 990s sometimes can be helpfully supplemented by an organization's annual report. It's voluntary and typically is addressed to the organization's financial contributors and other supporters. The 2011–12 report of the Metropolitan Opera Association Inc., for instance, included colorful pie charts showing breakdowns of the sources of its $324 million in total revenues and where its $327 million in operating expenses went. Interestingly, fundraising expenses totaled $15.4 million, 9.7 percent of operating contributions—a good insight into the massive effort needed to keep a major charitable organization afloat. While the IRS doesn't require public disclosure of an organization's donors, some not-for-profits like the Met voluntarily provide such information in their annual reports. The Met report lists thousands of donors, categorized by amounts ranging from $50 million-and-up to $600-and-up.

(Incidentally, it's worth noting here that ProPublica, the not-for-profit investigative news organization, wants to make clear that its major supporters' gifts don't constitute any conflict of interest that might water down ProPublica's reporting about them or their interests. So it publishes in its annual report the names of donors who contributed $50,000 or more each, more than 50 of them in 2014.)

Of course, not every not-for-profit organization possesses the financial muscle of these large, well-established institutions. In fact, there are thousands of 501(c)(3)s, as they're often called. Many of them have educational or charitable missions that are strictly local, and are carried out by making donations rather than by conducting operations, for instance, preserving green space or supporting public education or local museums or arts organizations. They may have an endowment that generates sufficient income to carry out that mission, so they don't need to conduct public fundraising campaigns and aren't really prominent in the community. But they all must file that annual Form 990, so if you have a quiet day occasionally, it might be worth your while to identify one or two of these local not-for-profits and check out their finances to see if anything has changed that might be worth a story. In particular, are revenues rising or falling significantly? If they engage in public fundraising, are those expenditures up or down recently, and are contributions changing commensurately? Are the organizations enlarging or shrinking their staffs? If you see changes, give them a call and find out why and whether their operations or donations are being altered accordingly. Also, there could be ripple effects, for better or worse, in the local charitable organizations that ordinarily receive the donations.

Questions for Discussion

1 If a not-for-profit doesn't post its Form 990 on its website and you can't access it through GuideStar, how might you obtain it?
2 Is it ethical to write about a quiet local not-for-profit, based on its Form 990, if it doesn't return your phone calls?
3 What signs might suggest that a local not-for-profit that conducts operations, such as a museum or a dance company, is in financial trouble warranting a look at its Form 990?

Conclusion
You're Important!

Whew! You've made it to the end! Congratulations! Of course, as the commencement speakers always remind the graduates, this isn't really the end, it's the beginning. But if you've tackled many of the business stories described in this book—not necessarily all of them—you've made the extra effort that most journalism students won't. That means you're ready to take on some of the most challenging, and most gratifying, jobs in journalism today. Why today? Because the peoples of the world, in our daily lives, are becoming increasingly internationalized, and much of that internationalization is economic and financial. A rising value of the dollar, unfortunately, makes our exports more expensive and puts a damper on American manufacturing, threatening jobs. On the other hand imports become cheaper, more affordable when we shop, for clothing or electronics, notably. The Trans Pacific Partnership agreement among the U.S. and other Pacific Rim nations promises to reduce barriers to trade, again meaning more affordable imports. American companies that merge or move abroad to lower their taxes are presumably strengthening their long-term prospects while, one would hope, not reducing their operations or employment in this country, maybe even enhancing them. (Of course it also means we taxpayers who remain here are probably going to have to pick up the slack—at least if our government ever moves toward balancing its budget.) Stock markets and derivatives markets around the world influence each other, and thus the values of our pension plans and personal investments here. When you plan to buy or sell, look first at what Asian and European markets did today.

And so it goes. Our democracy requires that journalists must follow and report these and other events that affect us and our government. It's increasingly complex. Clearly, financial journalists must undergo a modicum of education and training to tackle this task. And now you're among those ready to do it. You can take pride in what you've accomplished, a great leap forward. You can perform an important service to your nation as well as to the individuals who populate it, who play the diverse roles that make up our robust economy.

But a word of caution. As you become increasingly comfortable with the complexities of our economy, and the smart, sophisticated people who pull the strings—your sources—bear in mind that you're not one of them. You're still the dispassionate, disinterested observer of the markets and the economy. Your pursuit is greater than mastery of your challenging task. Your pursuit still is truth.

This simple mandate, unfortunately, is too easily ignored. In fact, we have witnessed three egregious lapses in business journalism in recent decades, each time allowing if not actually contributing to irrational euphoria that suddenly shattered, wreaking swift and catastrophic losses on business and investors and causing huge recovery costs imposed on the taxpayers by the same politicians who abetted the speculations. The causes, the precursors, of these terribly costly collapses all flowed from very public actions and decisions by government and by business. In reporting them routinely, with little or no skepticism or evaluation, the press was complicit in these disasters. It was too content to chronicle the nonsensically mushrooming wealth of instant millionaires, unsupportable market prices and the obsequious adoration of thinly capitalized businesses and start-up companies with no profits and sometimes even no sales or revenues.

The lesson? We need a smarter, more skeptical, more perceptive business press. It can well be argued that probing business journalists could have highlighted the publicly evident actions that would in time lead to these three catastrophes, and perhaps moderated or even averted their horrors. What happened? It's instructive to look at each of the three, all different, but all disastrous.

The Savings & Loan Debacle of the 1980s

This was a man-made crisis, a multiple failure of regulation, politics and the press. Until the 1980s the savings-and-loan business was steady, virtually risk-free, and thus lightly regulated, essentially by friendly regulators who were fervent advocates of the "American dream" of home ownership. S&Ls did what they were supposed to do: gather individual savings and use them to make home loans. The S&Ls, whether chartered by federal or state authorities, were mostly mutuals, owned by their depositors. There were no shares, no shareholders, no quarterly, public financial reports.

Until they got greedy. And found equally greedy politicians who were only too happy to do their bidding—for suitable rewards, of course. Eyeing the greater profits of commercial banks, S&Ls began converting to corporate form, issuing shares to their depositors, and lobbying legislators for greater powers. Congress acquiesced, and in a 1980 statute granted federally chartered S&Ls authority to make commercial (business) loans, to issue corporate bonds and credit cards, to remove the long-standing cap on savings interest rates, and to raise federal deposit insurance from $10,000 to $100,000, encouraging irresponsible management. Just two years later, in 1982, Congress again obliged, empowering S&Ls to borrow from deposit insurance funds, to engage in non-home lending, to offer bank-like checking accounts as well as the traditional savings accounts, and to permit ownership of S&Ls by non-financial companies. To top off their statutory gifts, Congress allowed federally chartered S&Ls to call themselves banks, "federal savings banks" to be precise, further obliterating the traditional (and worthy) distinction between the ultra-safe "thrifts" and somewhat riskier banks.

Then Congress passed the permissive baton to the S&L regulator, at that time the Federal Home Loan Bank Board. It followed suit. The Board permitted thrifts to be acquired by real estate developers, who had motives very different from those of traditional cautious thrift overseers. And that wasn't all, far from it. The Board also lowered thrifts' capital minimums from traditional levels of 7 or 8 percent of total assets to an unheard-of 4 percent, then 3 percent; counted acquisition "goodwill," an accounting figment, as capital along with real dollars; allowed bad loans sold to be counted as assets still held; permitted profits from phony "sales" of their buildings to be booked as capital; and, with bonds appreciating at the time, allowed the rising values of bond investments to be counted as capital.

With the rules relaxed, regulatory inspections were actually *reduced*. The results were predictable: deceptive accounting, fraud, mismanagement and lavish waste, risky lending, flimsy loans to insiders and hundreds of S&L failures, literally 10 percent of the total existing at the time.

Five U.S. senators, including John McCain, were so embarrassed by their influence peddling inside the government on behalf of one of the most infamous S&L wheeler-dealers, Charles Keating, that they actually returned millions in political donations received from his company.

The Tech Bubble of the 1990s

In the 1990s the stock market, as measured by the Standard & Poor's 500-Stock Index, quadrupled. The white-hot advance was led by technology-based stocks. The tech-heavy NASDAQ stock market soared by a multiple of *15*! Many small start-up companies with no profits went public, meaning they sold shares to the public for the first time, at unheard-of multiples of *revenues* (radically debased from the traditional measure of multiples of *earnings*, or profits), which analysts unaccountably "justified" as a fair measurement of the value of an unprofitable company. In 1995 alone a stock called General Magic went public at $14 and soared to $32 before the end of its first-day trading. Premisys Communications came out at $16, leapt to $36 and shortly to $52. Tivoli Systems launched at $13 and went promptly to $31, then $37. All are gone.

Even after the usually circumspect chairman of the Federal Reserve Board, Alan Greenspan, in 1996 declared the market obsessed with "irrational exuberance," it continued upward. In 1998 science and technology mutual funds jumped 51 percent, and the NASDAQ 100 Index sold for *100* times earnings compared with the traditional 18 or so. In the following year, America Online stock traded at *347* times earnings. In 1999, as the NASDAQ index advanced further to what would prove to be its peak, Qualcomm, a purveyor of wireless communications, gained *1700* percent.

Finally, with no thanks to the news media, the tide turned. Investors panicked. In 2000–2001 the S&P Index sank 37 percent, the NASDAQ 72 percent. In 2000 alone $2.4 trillion in market value was wiped out, meaning huge losses for millions of stockholders. The impact on individuals and families was calamitous. *USA Today* reported on a young father who lost $50,000 and was selling his tech stocks at huge losses to buy a car. *The St. Louis Post-Dispatch* said a man who had retired early on his stock markets profits, an incredible $1 million in 1999 alone, lost it all in 2000.

The Real Estate Debacle of the 2000s

Nevertheless, it didn't take long for investors to fall for another Wall Street flimflam. At the turn of the century people turned from stocks to real estate as defensive assets, and property values took off, at least in some parts of the country, such as Orange County, California. In 2002 *The Wall Street Journal* reported that home prices nationwide had risen at an attractive 6 percent a year since 1963.

Financiers saw an opportunity, and wasted no time in capitalizing on it. They created new bonds, called mortgage-backed securities, secured (backed) by large pools of mortgage loans, got top AAA ratings for the bonds, and sold them to investors seeking security as well as attractive yields. When the financiers, mostly investment bankers, ran out of mortgage loans, they lowered the standards and securitized adjustable-rate mortgages. Many of these featured very low come-on initial rates; they were being peddled by mortgage brokers to marginal borrowers who were led to believe that the appreciating value of the homes they were buying would enable them to refinance and reduce their monthly payments. In other words, the financiers peddled bonds secured by weak loans. Then the financiers bet against their own bonds by buying insurance, called credit default swaps, that would pay off if the mortgage borrowers defaulted. The government-chartered mortgage buyers, Fannie Mae and Freddie Mac, recently "privatized" and managed by politically connected incompetents, had been packaging mortgage loans and selling high-quality mortgage-backed bonds for years, all very prudently, successfully supporting the nationwide availability of mortgage financing. But now, concerned about losing market share, they followed the lower-standards lead of private mortgage packagers.

Soaring real estate prices finally reversed in 2007 as reality began to replace the years-long speculative fever. Suddenly mortgage defaults and then the failure of mortgage-backed securities threatened the entire economy. Home buyers defaulted en masse. American International Group, the principal seller of insurance against mortgage-bond defaults, was deemed by government regulators as too big to fail, and so got a bailout of $182 billion from the Treasury, i.e., from the taxpayers. Bear Stearns, mortally wounded by the failure of its mortgage-backed securities, sold itself for a song to JP Morgan. Lehman Bros. failed. The Treasury and the Federal Reserve persuaded Congress to appropriate $700 billion for the Troubled Asset Relief Program, a massive purchase of tottering securities. In fact the government committed even more than that, $787 billion, to include rescuing Citigroup and General Motors as well as Wall Street. Another $151 billion of taxpayer money was committed to the rescue and government takeover of the two giant government-chartered mortgage companies, Fannie Mae and Freddie Mac.

But the damage to the economy was done. What ensued was the worst economic downturn since the Great Depression in the 1930s. It was dubbed the Great Recession. The collapse of real estate values and Wall Street institutions led to mass forfeitures of mortgage loans and mortgage-backed securities, widespread unemployment and consumer reluctance to spend. The U.S. economy, particularly employment, struggled for five years to recover from the painful recession of 2008–2009.

Where Was the Press?

It must be restated and emphasized that all the irresponsible actions by government, financiers and the markets that caused the above debacles were totally public, commonly covered but too perfunctorily by the press.

For instance, in the 1980s S&L boom, the news media reported the relaxation of rules and standards, but didn't question their soundness, despite the deviation from time-honored sound banking and lending practices. It wasn't until 1989, just before the bubble burst, that *The Wall Street Journal*, angry at delays in closing bad S&Ls that doubled the taxpayers' cost, called for the head of the S&L regulator.

Late in the 1990s tech stock boom, the *Chicago Tribune* reported that "telecom horizons are unlimited," and the *Washington Post* bemoaned a "shortage" of tech stocks to invest in.

On the other hand, it must be noted that early in the 2000s real estate craze, *The Wall Street Journal*, to its credit, asked whether the meteoric inflation in real estate prices was "a bubble waiting to pop?" And *The New York Times* reported in 2004 on a Goldman Sachs study that found average home price overvalued by 10 percent.

Nevertheless, the prevailing press supported the notion of an endless boom. As late as 2005 the *Richmond Times Dispatch* published a recommendation to buy real estate "regardless of price," and *USA Today* said economists saw no national downturn and housing builders were irritated by "sky is falling" predictions.

Finally, in the last half of 2006, on the eve of the 2007 real estate reversal, the press did report a few dire comments: Economist Mark Zandi of Moody's was quoted as saying that the "housing peak was a year ago." Fabled bond manager Bill Gross of PIMCO remarked that housing was "not looking good." Economist Nouriel Roubini was reported as saying that it was "just a few months … before recession." And a U.S. Bank economist predicted a recession in 2007.

The Press Remiss

Why did it take the press, ferociously proud of its independence, so long to sense the dangers in these three buildups to catastrophe? Even when business journalists finally published cautious views, it was simply to quote established, authoritative voices. If the press had exercised truly independent judgment, it would have sensibly questioned Wall Street euphoria. The resulting stories would have unearthed contrarian views (they're always out there), compared incredible prices and values against historical standards, and called out securities analysts who suddenly veered from the traditional focus on price/earnings ratios to fuzzy "valuations" of companies that had never turned a profit.

A recent book by Dean Starkman, *The Watchdog That Didn't Bark: The Financial Crisis and the Disappearance of Investigative Journalism* (Columbia U. Press, 2014), about the coverage of the 2000s real estate debacle, accused business journalists of excessively practicing "access" reporting, which he said relied too much on cultivating friendly relationships with executives in big companies. Starkman alleged that this emphasis, with its concomitant desire to avoid offending business, "crowded out" investigative reporting which, in his view, might have nipped the crisis in the bud.

Whatever the reasons, the nation, and countless millions of individuals, paid a high price for all three of these speculative bubbles. Could an alert and skeptical press have prevented, or at least moderated, them? We'll never know.

However, this much is clear: if there was a single cause of the journalistic failings that preceded our last three economic catastrophes, it was the willingness of reporters to just go along with the developing bubbles, marveling uncritically at these uncommon events, and thus helping to inflate them beyond all historical reason. With disastrous consequences.

So think for yourself. Dare to be different! Just as there are always "contrarians" going against the flow in the stock market, there's always room for a different view of the economy and consumer sentiment in business journalism. This independent kind of journalism must be supported, of course, by facts, numbers and expert interpretation. So, when you have a hunch that your facts and numbers support such a divergent story, find experts who have that view. Explain why your facts, numbers and experts deserve consideration. You just might be right. That's the truth.

And above all, laugh every day!

Works Cited

Metropolitan Opera 2013 Annual Report:
www.metopera.org/uploadedFiles/MetOpera/annual%20reports/ANNUAL report%20FY13_FINAL.pdf

ProPublica 2014 Annual Report:
http://s3.amazonaws.com/propublica/assets/about/propublica-2014-annual-report.pdf?_ga=1.149758257.624353026.1414087525

Starkman, Dean, *The Watchdog That Didn't Bark: The Financial Crisis and the Disappearance of Investigative Journalism*, New York: Columbia University Press (2014).

Appendix

Can all the stories in this book realistically be undertaken by students? Yes, and here are a few fine examples written by students at Northwestern University's Medill School of Journalism, Media, Integrated Marketing Communications (all except the story by Joe Mathewson, author of this textbook, about University of Illinois athletics finances). These reporters are graduate students on the way to an MSJ degree, but there's no reason such original stories can't be reported and written by motivated undergraduates with basic journalism training and skills.

Who doesn't love a craft brewery, a fascinating local business even if you don't care for beer? A good story that exists everywhere these days is "Half Acre Beer to Expand After Reaching Capacity," by Paulo Cabral Filho.
http://news.medill.northwestern.edu/chicago/news.aspx?id=231098
(viewed Nov. 23, 2015)

A fine example of an imaginative and discerning consumer trend story based entirely on local interviewing is "Young TV Viewers Bypass Cable," by Aimee Keane.
http://newsarchive.medill.northwestern.edu/chicago/news-231291.html
(viewed Nov. 23, 2015)

A farm story with hard numbers, readily available from real estate agents if not farmers—a story that could be done in much of the country—treats the astonishing rise in the price of farmland. A good example by Ian Sawicki is "Heady Global Forces Fuel Farm Boom in Illinois."
http://newsarchive.medill.northwestern.edu/chicago/news-201500.html
(viewed Nov. 23, 2015)

An obscure professional sport and an athlete willing to talk about her pay and her life made a fine sports business story: "Pro Softball: Not a Lemonade Stand," by Elise Menaker.
http://newsarchive.medill.northwestern.edu/chicago/news-206205.html (viewed Nov. 23, 2015)

"March Madness: Big Bucks for Big Baskets in Illinois," by Joe Mathewson, is an illuminating, numbers-based examination of college sports financing that could be profitably undertaken in regard to almost any big state university.
http://chicagosidesports.com/march-madness-big-bucks-for-big-baskets-in-illinois/ (viewed Nov. 23, 2015)

"Lee County Turbines: Financial Windfall or Just Hot Air," by Marci Jacobs, is a thoughtful, multi-source examination of the common present-day tussle between farmers and public officials seeking additional income from ample rural acreage and conservationists who object to the noise, the appearance and the danger to birds of the huge windmills.
http://newsarchive.medill.northwestern.edu/chicago/news-223144.html (viewed Nov. 23, 2015)

"Possible Fraud in Caesars Bankruptcy Filing in Chicago," by Matt Yurus, is a clear explication of a complicated bankruptcy case enveloped in what some creditors alleged was a furtive and illicit removal of assets from the company before it filed.
http://news.medill.northwestern.edu/chicago/possible-fraud-an-issue-in-caesars-bankruptcy-filing-in-chicago/#more-9349 (viewed Nov. 23, 2015)

Index

adjusted earnings 28
agriculture story 96–100; agribusiness story 96–7; farmer story 97–9; questions for discussion 100; urban agriculture 99–100
American ingenuity 88–90
annual rate 70
appropriation bill 11
asset-backed commercial paper 17
asset managers (portfolio managers) 14
Associated Press (AP) style 12
attrition, verbs of 17–19
authorization bill 11

balance sheet 24, 38
bank holding company 11, 45
bankruptcy story 54–9; Chapter 7 liquidation 58; Chapter 9 bankruptcy 59; Chapter 11 bankruptcy 54–8; Chapter 13 bankruptcy 58; liquidation 54; petition for protection from creditors 54; questions for discussion 59; tips 59; wage-earner's bankruptcy 58
banks 44–6; bank holding company 45; chargeoffs 45; commercial bank 44; earnings streams 45–6; investment bank 44; net interest income 45; net interest margin 45; non-interest income 46; provision for credit losses 45; smaller banking companies 45–6; statement of condition, 46
base year 70
bond (debt) offering 51–3

bonds 86–7
budget authorization 11
business journalism, conclusion 111–17; journalistic failings 116–17; press coverage 115–16; real estate debacle (2000s) 115–16; savings & loan debacle (1980s) 112–13; tech bubble (1990s) 113–14
business journalism, introduction to 1–4; competition 2; hiding the truth 2; job opportunities 4; man on the street 3; story based on doubt 3–4
business organizations (words) 12–14; corporations 12–13; general partners 14; limited liability company 13; limited partners 14; partnership 13–14; personal liability 12; professional corporation 13; sole proprietorship 13; unincorporated businesses 13–14
buy side 39, 60

call report 39
capacity utilization 9
cascade of default 16
chain-type price index 11
Chapter 7 liquidation 58
Chapter 9 bankruptcy 59
Chapter 11 bankruptcy 54–8; Bankruptcy Court proceedings 55; bankruptcy trustee 55; company discharged from bankruptcy 57; cramdown 56; debtor in possession 55; debtor-in-possession financing 56; petition-filing story 55; plan of

122 Index

reorganization 56; Reorganization 54; reporting the story 57; story structure 57–8
Chapter 13 bankruptcy 58
chargeoffs 45
charitable organizations *see* not-for-profit story
Chicago Board of Trade 88
collateralized debt obligations (CDOs) 16, 91
college sports story 103
commercial bank 44
commercial paper 50
conference call 38–9
consultants 15
Consumer Confidence Index, 11
consumer price index (CPI) 11, 71
Consumer Sentiment Index 11
consumer spending 11
consumer story 83–7; bank accounts 84; bonds 86–7; exchange traded fund 86; fiscal policy 84; index fund 85; investments 84–7; monetary policy 84; mutual fund 85; questions for discussion 87; real estate investment trust 85; stock market 84
Core CPI 11
corporate finance story 50–3; bond (debt) offering 51–3; commercial paper 50; debt 50; equity 50; initial public offering 51; long-term liabilities 50; other liabilities 50; preferred stock 51; questions for discussion 53; rating agencies 52; short-term assets 50; stock offering 51; underwriter 51, 52
corporate officers 31–4; private companies 33–4; publicly held companies 31–3; still photos 33–4; video 34
corporate outlook story 60–8; analyst expectations 60–1; analyst report on stock 64; buy side 60; Earnings Before Interest, Taxes, Depreciation and Amortization 62; earnings forecasts 61–3; Generally Accepted Accounting Principles 61; lede 67; looking ahead 67; preparation 60–4; questions for discussion 68; rating the stock 61, 63; reporting the story 66; SEC filings 64–6; sell side 60; story structure 66–7; target price of stock 63; tips 68
corporations 12–13
cramdown 56
credit default swaps (CDS) 17
customer quote 78

debt 50
debtor-in-possession financing 56
deflation 8
derivatives story 88–95; American ingenuity 88–90; anomaly 93; calls 90; collateralized debt obligations 91; derivatives agonistes 91–2; exchange operations 94; financial futures 90; futures 88–90; lost jobs 94; mortgage-backed securities 91; options 90; problem derivatives 91–2; puts 90; quarterly earnings 94–5; questions for discussion 95; recycling the floor 94; remnants 94; stories 92–5; traders 92–3; Volatility Index 93
diluted figures 23
Dow Jones Industrial Average (DJIA) 9, 70

earnings 22
Earnings Before Interest, Taxes, Depreciation and Amortization (EBITDA) 28, 62
earnings story 37–43; analysts' earnings estimate 37; balance sheet 38; buy side 39; calling the securities analysts 37; clarification 39; closing price of stock 38; conference call 38–9; explanation 41–2; institutional investors 39; lede 40–1; net income (or earnings or profit) 38; note or call report 39; outlook 41; preparation 37–38; press release and financial statement 38; prior quarter's earnings story 38; questions for discussion 43; quotes 41; reporting 38–9; revenues (or sales) 38; securities analysts 39; sell side 39; statement of operations 38; stock 42; structure 40–2; tips 42–3

economic indicator story 69–73; annual rate 70; base year 70; compared to 70; consumer price index 71; Dow Jones Industrial Average 70; estimated number 69; index 70; nominal numbers 70; percentage points 70; preparation 69–71; questions for discussion 73; real numbers 70; reporting the story 71–2; revised number 69; seasonally adjusted figure 70; special terms 69–71; story structure 72; tips 72
economists 15
economy (words) 8–12; appropriation bill 11; authorization bill 11; bank holding companies 11; budget authorization 11; capacity utilization 9; chain-type price index 11; Consumer Confidence Index, 11; consumer price index 11; Consumer Sentiment Index 11; consumer spending 11; Core CPI 11; deflation 8; Dow Jones Industrial Average 9; Federal Open Market Committee 10; Federal Reserve Board 10; Federal Reserve System 10; fiscal policy 11; fiscal year 11; frictional unemployment 10; GDP price deflator 11; Great Recession 8; gross domestic product 8; housing starts 9; industrial production 9; investment banking 11; market, the 9; monetary policy 10; NASDAQ Composite Index 9; national debt 9; new-home sales 9; nominal GDP 9; personal consumption expenditures index 11; personal income 11; personal savings rate 12; quantitative easing 10; real GDP 8; recession 8; Russell 2000 Index 9; sales of existing homes 9; Standard & Poor's 500-Stock Index 9; unemployment rate 9
energy story 104–6; facilities management story 105; government pollution-control story 104–5; industry pollution-control story 105–6; questions for discussion 106; regulatory story 104–5
equity 50
equity analysts 14
estimated number 69
exchange traded fund (ETF) 86

Fannie Mae 16
farmer story 97–9
Federal Deposit Insurance Corporation 84
Federal Open Market Committee 10
Federal Reserve Board (the Fed) 10
Federal Reserve System 10
financial services reporting, 44–9; banks 44–46; insurance companies 46–7; questions for discussion 49; real estate investment trusts 47–9
financial statement 21–7; balance sheet 24; diluted figures 23; earnings 22; Generally Accepted Accounting Principles 22; goodwill 27; impairment 27; long-term liabilities 24; market capitalization 24; net income 22; net income attributable to common stockholders 22; net income per diluted share 23; net income per share 22; operating expenses 22; per share of common stock, number expressed as 22; profit 22; revenues 22; sales 22; short-term liabilities 24; statement of operations 22; stock-option compensation 22; stockholders' equity 24; subsidiary 27; vital numbers 22–6
fiscal policy 11, 84
fiscal year 11
Fitch 52
fixed-income analysts 14
flimsy loans 16
Freddie Mac 16
frictional unemployment 10
Funds From Operations (FFO) 48
futures contract 88

general partners 14
Generally Accepted Accounting Principles (GAAP) 22, 28, 47, 61
glitches (misuses of words) 19–20; adjusted earnings 19; bank 19; bankrupt 20; compared to 19; percent 19; secondary offering 19; spinoff 19

goodwill 27
government pollution-control story 104–5
Great Recession 8
gross domestic product (GDP) 8, 81, 83

housing starts 9

impairment 27
importance of business journalism 5–7; employers 5; questions for discussion 7; thriving nature of business journalism 5–7; training 5
index 70
index fund 85
industrial production 9
industry pollution-control story 105–6
initial public offering (IPO) 51
institutional investors 14, 39
insurance companies 46–7; combined ratio 47; dividend ratio 47; expense ratio 47; loss ratio 47; underwriters, 46
investment bank 44
investments, 84–7; bank accounts 84; bonds 86–7; exchange traded fund 86; fiscal policy 84; index fund 85; monetary policy 84; mutual fund 85; questions for discussion 87; real estate investment trust 85; stock market 84

journalistic failings 116–17

labor union actions 35
lede 40–1, 67
limited liability company (LLC) 13
limited partners 14
liquidation 54
long-term liabilities 24, 50

market, the 9
market capitalization 24
misuses of words 19–20
monetary policy 10, 84
Moody's Investors Service 52
mortgage-backed securities (MBS) 16, 91
mutual fund 85

NASDAQ stock market 51, 113
national debt 9
net income 22, 38
net income attributable to common stockholders 22
net income per diluted share 23
net income per share 22
net interest income 45
net interest margin 45
new-home sales 9
New York Stock Exchange 51
nominal GDP 9
nominal numbers 70
non-interest income 46
not-for-profit story 107–10; endowment 109; questions for discussion 110; tax exemptions 107
numbers 21–30; analysts' expectations 29–30; expert interpretation 29; financial statement 21–27; press release 27–9; questions for discussion 30

operating expenses 22
option on stocks 90

partnership 13–14
people 31–6; corporate officers, 31–4; labor union actions 35; other people 34–5; questions for discussion 36; random interviews 35
per share of common stock, number expressed as 22
personal consumption expenditures index 11
personal income 11
personal liability 12
personal savings rate 12
petition for protection from creditors 54
photos 76
portfolio managers 14
preferred stock 51
press release 27–9; adjusted earnings 28; dissimulation 28; Earnings Before Interest, Taxes, Depreciation and Amortization 28; explanations 28; quotations 29
professional corporation (PC) 13
professors 15
profit 22

Index

quantitative easing 10
quarterly earnings 94–5
questions for discussion: agriculture story 100; bankruptcy story 59; consumer story 87; corporate finance story 53; corporate outlook story 68; derivatives story 95; earnings story 43; economic indicator story 73; energy story 106; financial services reporting 49; importance of business journalism 7; not-for-profit story 110; numbers 30; people 36; small business story 79; sports business story 103; trend story 82; words 20
quotations 29
quotes 76–7

random interviews 35
real estate debacle (2000s) 115–16
real estate investment trusts (REITs) 47–9, 85; assets 48; Funds From Operations 48; peculiarity 47; real numbers 70
real GDP 8
recession 8
Reorganization (bankruptcy) 54
revenues 22, 38
revised number 69
Russell 2000 Index 9

sales 22, 38
sales of existing homes 9
savings & loan debacle (1980s) 112–13
seasonally adjusted figure 70
securities, troubled *see* troubled (and troubling) securities
securities analysts 14, 39
Securities and Exchange Commission (SEC) filings, 64–6; Form 8-K 65; Form 10-K 64; Form 10-Q 64–5; Form 13D 65–6; Form 14-A 65; Form 14D1F 66; Form 144 66
sell side 39, 60
short-term assets 50
short-term liabilities 24
small business story 74–9; customer quote 78; essence of story 78; history 78; missteps 77; numbers 75; other sources 77; photos/videos 76; preparation 74–5; questions for discussion 79; quotes 76–7; reporting the story 75–7; story structure 77–8
sole proprietorship 13
sources for business stories 14–15; asset managers (portfolio managers) 14; consultants 15; economists 15; equity analysts 14; fixed-income analysts 14; institutional investors 14; professors 15; securities analysts 14; trade and professional associations 15; trade publication editors and reporters 15
sports business story 101–3; athlete story 101; college sports story 103; fan story 101–2; private sports-dependent business story 102–3; public-company story 102; questions for discussion 103
Standard & Poor's 9, 52
statement of condition 46
statement of operations 22, 38
stock market 84
stock offering 51
stockholders' equity 24
stock-option compensation 22
subprime loans 16
subprime mortgage loans 16
subsidiary 27

tax exemptions 86, 107
tech bubble (1990s) 113–14
trade and professional associations 15
trade publication editors and reporters 15
trend story 80–2; experts 81; great quote 82; "however" graf 82; national trends 81; preparation 80–81; questions for discussion 82; quotes and numbers 81–2; story structure 81–2
troubled (and troubling) securities 16–17; asset-backed commercial paper 17; cascade of default 16; collateralized debt obligations 16; credit default swaps 17; flimsy loans 16; mortgage-backed securities 16; subprime mortgage loans 16

underwriter: insurance 46; investment bank acting as 51, 52
unemployment rate 9
unincorporated businesses 13–14
urban agriculture 99–100

verbs of attrition 17–19
videos 34, 76
vocabulary *see* words
Volatility Index (VIX) 93

wage-earner's bankruptcy 58
words 8–20; business organizations 12–14; economy 8–12; glitches (misuses of words) 19–20; sources for business stories 14–15; troubled (and troubling) securities 16–17; verbs of attrition 17–19